CONTENTS

TABLES AND FIGURES

PROGRESS IN TRADE FACILITATION IN CAREC COUNTRIES

A 10-YEAR CORRIDOR PERFORMANCE MEASUREMENT AND MONITORING PERSPECTIVE

DECEMBER 2022

© 2022 Asian Development Bank
6 ADB Avenue, Mandaluyong City, 1550 Metro Manila, Philippines
Tel +63 2 8632 4444; Fax +63 2 8636 2444
www.adb.org

Some rights reserved. Published in 2022.

ISBN 978-92-9269-854-6 (print); 978-92-9269-855-3 (electronic); 978-92-9269-856-0 (ebook)
Publication Stock No. TCS220519-2
DOI: http://dx.doi.org/10.22617/TCS220519-2

Notes:
In this report, "$" refers to United States dollars.
ADB recognizes "China" as the People's Republic of China.

On the cover: Crude Storage Tank at Zuun Khatavch border (photo by Andy Sze); the Customs Clearance Zone at Poti, Georgia (photo by Max Ee); Black Sea Ferry at Batumi (photo by Andy Sze); the toll plaza at the entrance of E-35 Hassanabdal-Havelian Expressway from Peshawar Motorway (photo by Nasr ur Rahman/ADB); daily life, architecture and views of Tashkent (photo by Relisa Granovskaya/ADB); cargo and passenger transport inspection at the Khorgos Customs Post in Almaty Region, Kazakhstan—People's Republic of China Border Zone (photo by Andrey Terekhov/ADB); Uygur children at old Kashgar (photo by Andy Sze); Afghan porter loads potatoes on the truck in Bamian city, Afghanistan (photo by Jawad Jalali/ADB); a wagon transporting grains at Aktau seaport (photo by Max Ee).

Cover design by Chris Fischer.

FOREWORD

Since the report's inception in 2009, the Corridor Performance Measurement and Monitoring (CPMM) has proven to be a useful tool for quantifying and monitoring the efficacy of transport corridors, using private sector data of actual commercial shipments along the Central Asia Regional Economic Cooperation (CAREC) corridors. It allows CAREC members* to measure their performance on trade facilitation and learn new practices that have worked elsewhere. It has informed dialogue, collaboration, and decision-making by the 11 member countries of the CAREC Program on trade facilitation.

CPMM was launched in 2010 as part of the CAREC Transport and Trade Facilitation Strategy 2020 adopted in 2008, which was then superseded by the CAREC Transport Strategy 2030 approved in 2019 and the CAREC Integrated Trade Agenda 2030 approved in 2018. CPMM's aim has been to collate, analyze, and evaluate empirical time and cost data on commercial shipments transported along the six CAREC corridors. The use of data provided by drivers and freight forwarders of actual shipments and verified by national transport and/or trade associations makes CPMM a reliable tool for measuring performance and identifying bottlenecks and friction along the corridors—especially at border crossings—and for determining why shipment times and costs are sometimes higher than they need to be. Results from the CAREC CPMM can fill gaps in research on regional trade facilitation initiatives and have supplemented the outputs of the World Customs Organization's Time Release Studies and the United Nations Educational, Scientific and Cultural Organization's Business Process Analysis. These also measure time and cost of goods spent at borders, but at select few border-crossing points and at irregular intervals.

CPMM findings and conclusions, which are reported at each annual CAREC ministerial conference, have become broader and more granular over time. Road and transport time and cost data are now disaggregated and based on separate lists of the different border-crossing activities involved. Functionality was added to cover multimodal shipments such as those transported across the Caspian Sea or by both road and rail in Mongolia. Although performance was initially assessed by corridors alone, CPMM data are now available for evaluations by country and by individual border-crossing points. Each CPMM annual report contains a CAREC case study with a trade facilitation theme. CPMM development took another major step in 2020 when the Asian Development Bank (ADB) and the CAREC Institute began working together to promote and further enhance the methodology of data collection and reporting, as well as advocacy. This joint work led to a series of recommendations for expanding the objectives and upgrading the methods and tool kits of CPMM, implementation of which began in 2021.

---

* The CAREC Program is a partnership of 11 countries—Afghanistan, Azerbaijan, the People's Republic of China, Georgia, Kazakhstan, the Kyrgyz Republic, Mongolia, Pakistan, Tajikistan, Turkmenistan, and Uzbekistan—working together to promote development through cooperation, leading to accelerated economic growth and poverty reduction. See CAREC. www.carecprogram.org. ADB placed on hold its assistance in Afghanistan effective 15 August 2021.

This publication offers a longitudinal 10-year perspective on trends and impediments in trade facilitation across the CAREC countries. The level of detail in the publication is out of the ordinary, with analyses based on more than 2,000 samples a year, and bottlenecks in CAREC cross-border trade pinpointed along with their specific causes. The publication covers the impacts of major events, particularly the coronavirus disease (COVID-19) outbreak, and provides projections and recommendations for a full recovery, and faster and more efficient growth of CAREC countries' trade in the years ahead.

The CPMM modality demonstrated its value during the pandemic. National statistics could show how trade dipped in 2020 and rebounded in 2021, but not highlight the enduring challenges faced by international shippers and transport operators at specific locations along each CAREC corridor and how these were or remain to be addressed. Continued promotion and strengthening of CPMM is made even more indispensable by fragility and vulnerabilities in the recovery of international trade and supply chains, a recovery that has been disrupted by the Russian invasion of Ukraine. CPMM data and insights will continue to provide fact-based information critical to trade facilitation.

We trust that CAREC policy makers and stakeholders will consider CPMM findings and recommendations and apply them when formulating policies and regulations to eliminate the institutional and regulatory barriers that impede the efficient flow of goods across the region. Removing these obstacles will pave the way for the people of the CAREC countries to prosper as the region becomes an ever smoother and more efficient part of a land bridge across the Eurasian continent.

M. Teresa Kho
Director General
East Asia Department

Yevgeniy Zhukov
Director General
Central and West Asia Department

ABBREVIATIONS

ADB	Asian Development Bank
AEO	authorized economic operator
BCP	border-crossing point
CAR	Central Asian Republic
CAREC	Central Asia Regional Economic Cooperation
CBTA	Cross-Border Transport Agreement
CCZ	customs clearance zone
CPMM	Corridor Performance Measurement and Monitoring
EAEU	Eurasian Economic Union
GDP	gross domestic product
GRS	Georgia Revenue Service
PRC	People's Republic of China
QTTA	Quadrilateral Traffic in Transit Agreement
RIBS	Regional Improvement of Border Services
SPS	sanitary and phytosanitary
SWD	speed with delay
SWOD	speed without delay
TFI	trade facilitation indicator
TIR	Transports Internationaux Routiers (International Road Transports)
WTO	World Trade Organization

WEIGHTS AND MEASURES

kg	kilogram
km	kilometer
km/h	kilometers per hour
mm	millimeter
TEU	twenty-foot equivalent unit

EXECUTIVE SUMMARY

The Central Asia Regional Economic Cooperation (CAREC) Program is a multilateral platform that promotes and facilitates regional cooperation, connectivity, and integration between 11 member countries. This publication describes the progress made by the program's trade facilitation efforts from 2010 to 2020. The Corridor Performance Measurement and Monitoring (CPMM) is a mature methodology to quantify, evaluate, and monitor the time- and cost-efficiency of cross-border trade across six CAREC corridors. The CPMM was conceptualized and tested in 2009 and officially launched in 2010. This publication describes the evolution of CPMM, refinement of its methodology, and its application to identify bottlenecks to provide a full picture of the progress on trade facilitation in the CAREC region.

The CAREC Program has made great strides toward closer cooperation among its member countries over this period. Discussions have occurred on such regional initiatives as the Cross-Border Transport Agreement, the Quadrilateral Transit Trade Agreement, and the CAREC Advanced Transit System. The CAREC Customs Cooperation Committee serves as the regional platform for enhancing customs cooperation and helped bring about the adoption of the Revised Kyoto Convention. The CAREC countries have also collaborated on sanitary and phytosanitary matters and agreed to the common use of electronic phyto certificates.

Transport and trade face particularly difficult natural obstacles in the CAREC region. Eight of the countries are landlocked and far from major blue-water ports. This and their often-inadequate infrastructure have placed major time and cost constraints on moving goods to and from international markets. Other barriers are institutional, as CPMM findings highlight, and these create trade friction, limit market access, and stifle economic opportunities between CAREC members and their near neighbors. For example, the South Asian countries'* share of the overall value of all exports from the five Central Asian republics has hovered at only about 3% for a decade. This persists despite the proximity of the two regions and the existence of complementary trade and economic needs.

Many important international and regional developments during 2010–2020 have had significant implications for the CAREC countries. In particular, the rise of container express trains linking the Eurasian continent showed that when regional cooperation and connectivity are in place, remarkable achievements can happen. It is possible now to ship merchandise from East Asia to Europe in 12 days, faster than ocean freight and cheaper than air freight.

This publication also describes the impact of the coronavirus disease (COVID-19) pandemic that disrupted businesses and international trade in 2020. The general control and sanitary measures

---

* Afghanistan, Bangladesh, Bhutan, India, Maldives, Nepal, Pakistan, and Sri Lanka.

taken in the region and the individual actions taken by each CAREC member country are discussed. An immediate impact was a deterioration in the trade facilitation indicators measured and estimated by CPMM in 2019–2020.

Border-crossing time for both road and rail transport increased during the pandemic. The delays were caused by longer waiting and processing time due to additional and stricter implementation of controls, as well as closures of road border points, particularly at the beginning of the pandemic. While the border-crossing cost for road transport increased due to additional epidemiological measures and quarantine actions, rail transport did not experience such problems. In fact, since railways were the lifeline for food and medical supplies when road border points were closed, costs dropped as governments lowered related fees and simplified charges.

From 2010 to 2020, the average time and cost to travel through CAREC corridors by road and rail showed limited progress. Shipments still face delays and fees at borders. Restrictions that prevent foreign-registered vehicles from crossing borders are a major constraint and can cause delays. Freight are required to be offloaded from one truck and reloaded onto another. Vehicle and train transport speeds also suffered to varying degrees due to trip interruptions at police checkpoints and congestion at border crossings.

However, the average overall CAREC region estimates mask the progress made by individual countries. Performance varied greatly, and many countries have consistently improved border-crossing times since 2010. These improvements, however, were offset by the lack of progress or even deterioration in efficiency in a few countries, whose border-crossing time was far higher than the regional average. Similarly, CPMM data also revealed a decline in the costs incurred to cross a border either by road or rail in most countries. However, persistent high costs in a few countries drove up the regional average. This suggests that efforts to improve risk management, streamline border control procedures, and enhance connectivity proved effective in many countries, but CAREC members are at different stages in terms of implementing these measures. Continued efforts and improvements are required to lift the regional performance as a whole.

This publication lists the main trade impediments that need attention and resolution. Being landlocked and lack of access to seaports are geographical constraints for many CAREC countries. More importantly, policy impediments, including lack of economic diversification, transit challenges, and border-crossing complexities, undermine the smooth flow of freight. These have led to high transport costs, documentation challenges, and slow shipment speeds, which prove unfavorable to shippers in international trade. In addition, institutional barriers such as unharmonized standards (e.g., on food safety) and corruption remain structural and significant. With empirical data from CPMM utilized to support assertions made, this publication elaborates on some key initiatives that are expected to improve trade facilitation.

The CAREC Program, in consultation with its member countries, has formulated actions to address the issues underlying these constraints. Among these efforts are the new Transport Strategy 2030 and the CAREC Integrated Trade Agenda 2030, two key strategic plans to support CAREC member countries. They seek to expand cross-border transport and logistics infrastructure to address capacity constraints such as the Regional Improvement in Border Services projects. The harmonization of transport and vehicle standards could address the need at borders to transload shipments between trucks, a practice that CPMM identified as a key problem.

Enhancing customs transparency and coordinating border-crossing operations would go a long way to improve border-crossing performance. On top of this, an authorized economic operator system could be instituted nationally and then regionally—if the CAREC members could harmonize their standards. This would address current at-the-border and behind-the-border impediments. Trains would need expanded capacity as a cost-effective transport mode as freight is expected to continue to divert from air, ocean, and road due to the pandemic and the global supply chain disruption. The development of freight trains or container express trains could be a measure to relieve the global cargo congestion in ocean freight and reduce transport costs.

The outlook for regional trade in the CAREC region is examined in a separate chapter. First, new transport or economic corridors are expected to emerge in addition to the six existing CAREC corridors formalized in 2005–2006. A Shymkent–Tashkent–Khujand economic corridor is one example. CPMM has detected an increase in trade flows between the People's Republic of China (PRC), Tajikistan, and Afghanistan through the Kulma Pass which potentially indicates emergence of alternative routes from the PRC to Central Asia and South Asia. Second, elevated ocean freight rates are expected to continue for an extended period to incentivize the shipment of goods by train. The global ocean freight index has surged to unprecedented levels, and the cost to ship a 40-foot container from Shanghai to Rotterdam by sea stood at more than $13,000 in August 2021, seven times the pre-pandemic level. This rate subsequently decreased in 2022 to $3,688 in October 2022. A third projection is that digitalization will open many new commercial opportunities. Teleconferencing tools, the Internet of Things, and other innovations are projected to move businesses toward Industry 4.0. Due to the recent accession to the Transports Internationaux Routiers (TIR) or International Road Transports Convention by Pakistan and the PRC, the use of TIR is predicted to increase. Finally, cross-border e-commerce is described as another trend to watch. The growing number of retail and business buyers purchasing items online will likely continue to recast the transport business.

Country-level analysis has long been a part of the CPMM annual report, and this publication provides key trade facilitation indicator data for each CAREC member country. The time and costs of transporting through each border-crossing point under study are also reported. CPMM has collected a large sample of data based on actual commercial shipments over the past decade. This data can be helpful to national policy makers, and CPMM will continue to explore new innovative ways to utilize this data productively.

In summary, CAREC countries have taken significant steps to improve regional cooperation and connectivity, and to facilitate trade, but many challenges—and opportunities—remain to be addressed. Achieving success in doing so would enable the CAREC region to become an essential land bridge and land link for global trade. This publication identifies important structural barriers standing in the way and prescribes possible actions to remove them.

In the end, political will is the single most important factor in determining whether the necessary measures will be taken and where CAREC region countries will be when the second CPMM perspective is published 10 years from now. In the meantime, the Asian Development Bank and the CAREC Program will remain committed partners in pursuing a more connected, prosperous, and unified region across Central Asia.

INTRODUCTION 1

Background

The Central Asia Regional Economic Cooperation (CAREC) Program includes 11 member countries: Afghanistan, Azerbaijan, Georgia, Kazakhstan, the Kyrgyz Republic, Mongolia, Pakistan, the People's Republic of China (PRC), Tajikistan, Turkmenistan, and Uzbekistan. CAREC member countries have different economic and trade profiles, as well as heritage and culture. Yet one common theme connects these countries—the interest to integrate with international trade systems and corridors so that their citizens can enjoy the benefits of inclusive and sustainable growth. As developing countries, they face constraints in physical and institutional barriers. This is what regional cooperation, facilitated by platforms such as CAREC, aims—to bring together these countries to review, discuss, and implement actions to address the challenges. A key outcome is to raise the level of regional cooperation to boost the countries' trade levels.[1]

Trade could be increased through trade policy liberalization (Drabek and Laird 2001) and trade facilitation (UNCTAD 2016). Trade policy, such as accession to the World Trade Organization (WTO) and joining multilateral trade agreements, aims to reduce trade barriers, encourage reciprocal treatment, and alleviate protectionist measures for the ultimate benefit of the consumers. However, in the transition process, the entry of foreign competitors and the lowering of import duties, for instance, imply a limited time window for national enterprises to raise their productivity and competitiveness. Failing this, they can become a victim of such liberalization.

Trade facilitation ensures the smooth flow of goods along trade routes. In the process of simplifying, standardizing, and harmonizing practices and procedures (Wilson, Mann, and Otsuki 2005), CAREC countries can eliminate or reduce conflict in cross-border trade. Initiatives such as trade and transport facilitation (e.g., transit trade agreement and road transit system) and customs (e.g., automated customs information system, national single window, and joint border cooperation) tend to reduce the time and cost for border crossings, thus, improving the efficiency of the supply chain. The CAREC initiative on Corridor Performance Measurement and Monitoring (CPMM) has provided empirical evidence on the gradual decline in time and cost indicators in CAREC countries over the past decade.[2]

---

[1] This report was prepared based on information available as of 31 July 2021.

[2] CPMM publishes technical a document annually, and for the benefit of readers, it includes standard explanations and definitions that are included in this report. Findings, recommendations, tables, and figures contain standard and recurring descriptions and names of border-crossing points and should remain consistent with previous annual reports.

Since 2010, the CAREC region has experienced many significant changes. This report describes the issues and developments in CAREC, highlighting the roles and impact of trade and transport facilitation. Despite deep-rooted and structural impediments, member countries achieved commendable progress, some aided by international donor organizations.[3]

Importance of Trade Facilitation in CAREC

The CAREC region is strategically located in the Eurasian continent. If the region can overcome the constraints of being landlocked to becoming land-linked, the enhanced regional connectivity will usher in new commercial opportunities, increasing trade and employment. Greater trade can attract more investment into infrastructure and service providers, leading to reduced shipment cost and time, which encourages further economic integration (Pomfret 2019). On the other hand, impediments such as "complicated tariff structures, customs procedures, cabotage, and other rules and procedures inhibiting smooth logistics" (Kalyuzhnova and Holzhacker 2021, p. 2) are particularly significant issues among the CAREC countries.

The WTO defines trade facilitation as the simplification, modernization, and harmonization of export and import processes.[4] Trade facilitation is one of the four focal areas under the CAREC strategic framework. The CAREC Program supports modernization and reforms through initiatives at the institutional level (e.g., Customs Cooperation Committee) and technical assistance to improve trade facilitation. These efforts target to reduce transport costs and time. With greater harmonization, standardization, and simplification, goods will spend less time waiting for permits, crossing the border, and completing the clearance process. Considering that most CAREC countries are transit nations for their neighbors, improved outcomes from enhanced trade facilitation will shorten the economic distance between origins and destinations.

Role of the CPMM

CPMM is a tool developed by the Asian Development Bank (ADB) for quantifying and monitoring the efficacy of transport corridors, using private sector data collection of actual commercial shipments along the CAREC corridors. The time and cost data from standardized forms are submitted monthly, which are subsequently aggregated, analyzed, and reported. CPMM uses four main trade facilitation indicators (TFIs): (i) time to cross a border, (ii) cost to cross a border, (iii) total transport cost, and (iv) speeds. The analysis is decomposed into road and rail transport, and "at the border" and "behind border."

---

[3] A comprehensive list of investment programs supported by ADB under the CAREC Program are published in the CAREC Transport Strategy and CAREC Transport and Trade Facilitation Strategy 2020; ADB. 2020. *CAREC Transport Strategy 2030*. Manila; and ADB. 2014. *CAREC Transport and Trade Facilitation Strategy 2020*. Manila.

[4] World Trade Organization. *Trade Facilitation*. https://www.wto.org/english/tratop_e/tradfa_e/tradfa_e.htm (accessed 13 August 2021).

It is essential to highlight that CPMM uses empirical data to estimate TFIs. Drivers provide the time and cost to complete the shipment, particularly the border-crossing operations. Freight forwarders submit the data for shipments on railways. National transport associations are contracted as CPMM partners to provide technical support, review, and verify the data as a control measure. Thus, the quality of the data collected offers more empirical evidence compared to survey methodologies that utilize perceptions. For this reason, CPMM is now widely cited as a reference to report on corridor performance, node-specific time and cost (e.g., border-crossing points [BCPs]), and comparisons of improvements over a time series.[5]

Objectives and Structure of the Report

This report aims to

(i)   Review the developments, issues, and progress in trade facilitation within the CAREC region during 2010–2020 and assess any improvements or deterioration in that period.

(ii)   Identify the key impediments creating friction in the cross-border movement of goods and explain which impediments have been addressed and which remain obstacles needing further attention from policy makers.

(iii)   Highlight improvements by some countries on cross-border trade and distill learning for other countries to consider applying these to their contexts.

(iv)   Evaluate the trade facilitation performance of each CAREC member country.

(v)   Identify the impacts of the COVID-19 pandemic and the near- and long-term ramifications of border-crossing controls for regional cooperation.

The publication presents a holistic perspective over time of the development of trade facilitation by drawing on the topics and analyses from past CPMM annual reports and synthesizing the key observations, commentaries, insights, findings, and data they contained. Investment programs and regional or national initiatives often take years to complete and have their full effect. A longer-term view and examination of subsequent developments are needed to fully determine the impact of legislative changes, bilateral and multilateral cooperation, and the modernization of a border-crossing point. This publication provides such a longer-term view and assessments not always possible in CPMM's individual annual reports.

Following the introduction in Chapter 1, Chapter 2 analyzes regional trends and performance from the CPMM perspective, drawing from a long series of indicators it tracks. It also briefly discusses key initiatives that have helped reshape the trade facilitation landscape in CAREC. It also discussed the impacts on the supply chain of the COVID-19 pandemic.

---

[5]   Many studies employ CPMM data to fill the gap in econometric models for transport and trade facilitation. Examples include A. Iimi. 2022. Estimating the Impacts of Transport Corridor Development in Kazakhstan: Application of Dynamic Panel Data Models to Firm Registry Data (English). *Policy Research Working Paper* No. WPS 10196 Washington, DC: The World Bank Group; and K. Kim and P. Mariano. 2020. Trade Impact of Reducing Time and Costs at Borders in the Central Asia Regional Economic Cooperation Region. *ADBI Working Paper* 1106. Tokyo: Asian Development Bank Institute.

Chapter 3 focuses on the impediments creating friction when goods move along the supply chains. This chapter concentrates less on the natural and geographical constraints in the region than on the institutional and policy barriers. In general, these include institutional elements (such as legislation, policies, and organizational design), transportation systems, economic structures, and regulations and procedures.

Chapter 4 briefly reviews the efforts by CAREC countries, evaluates the progress made, and identifies the areas needing further attention. It describes the extent and scope of ADB investment and technical assistance, which covers infrastructure, equipment, capacity, and institution building.

Chapter 5 discusses the outlook, looking at changes that can reshape current economic and trade patterns and further promote trade facilitation in the CAREC region. This includes development of post-pandemic supply chains and new emerging transport corridors and greater use of digitalization.

Chapter 6 presents recommendations for policy makers and international development partners.

REGIONAL TRENDS AND DEVELOPMENTS

2

CPMM Indicators

CPMM evaluates a set of four trade facilitation indicators (TFIs) to illustrate the overall annual performance and efficiency of the CAREC corridors.[6] Measured over time and across corridors, the indicators provide a comparative picture that allows the assessment and validation of impacts of transport and trade initiatives in the region. The four aggregate TFIs are as follows:

1. **TFI1: Time taken to clear a BCP.** This TFI refers to the average length of time (in hours) taken to move cargo across a border from the entry to the exit point of a BCP. The entry and exit points are typically primary control centers where customs, immigration, and quarantine are handled. Along with the standard clearance formalities, this measurement includes waiting time, unloading and loading time, time taken to change rail gauges, and other indicators. The intent is to capture both the complexity and the inefficiencies inherent in the border-crossing process.

2. **TFI2: Cost incurred at a BCP.** This is the average total cost, in United States (US) dollars, of moving cargo across a border from entry to exit of a BCP. Both official and unofficial payments are included.

3. **TFI3: Cost incurred to travel a corridor section.** This comprises the average total cost, in US dollars, incurred for one unit of cargo traveling along a corridor section within a country or across borders. One unit of cargo refers to a cargo truck or train carrying 20 tons of goods. A corridor section is defined as a stretch of road 500 kilometers (km) long. Both official and unofficial payments are included. However, in practice, due to data collection constraints, transport cost figures reported in CPMM refer to either transport rates for trucks or railway tariffs for trains.[7]

4. **TFI4: Speed to travel along CAREC corridors.** This is the average speed, in kilometers per hour (km/h), at which a unit of cargo travels along a corridor section within a country or across borders. A unit of cargo refers to a cargo truck or train carrying 20 tons of goods, and a corridor section refers to a stretch of road 500 km long. Speed is calculated by dividing the total distance traveled by the duration of travel. Distance and time measurements include border crossings.

---

[6] The TFIs are explained in CPMM annual reports, including statistical derivations. ADB. 2021. *CAREC Corridor Performance Measurement and Monitoring: Annual Report 2020— THE Coronavirus Disease and its Impact*. Manila.

[7] "Transport cost" is viewed from the perspective of the shipper and/or receiver. It represents the market rate paid to move the cargo, rather than the carrier's cost of providing the service.

Time and Cost in CAREC Trade

Figures 2.1 to 2.4 depict the average time and cost to cross BCPs by road and by rail. These show limited progress in reducing the average time and costs in cross-border points over the past decade. Shipment time in Central Asia tends to be lengthy and costly due to restrictions on foreign-registered vehicles crossing the border. This is particularly prevalent between Central Asian republics (CARs), and East Asia and South Asia. For example, the PRC trucks are stopped at the border and are typically not permitted to cross unless they carry a special bonded-truck license. Afghanistan and Pakistan trucks are similarly stopped at the Central Asian border due to the absence of the necessary road pass, which is difficult to secure. All these resulted in the need to transload freight between trucks at the border, thus adding significant delays to delivery.

Information on the average time and cost in border crossing masks the dynamism at the individual countries, whose performance varied greatly. On the border-crossing time, Figures 2.5 to 2.6 show

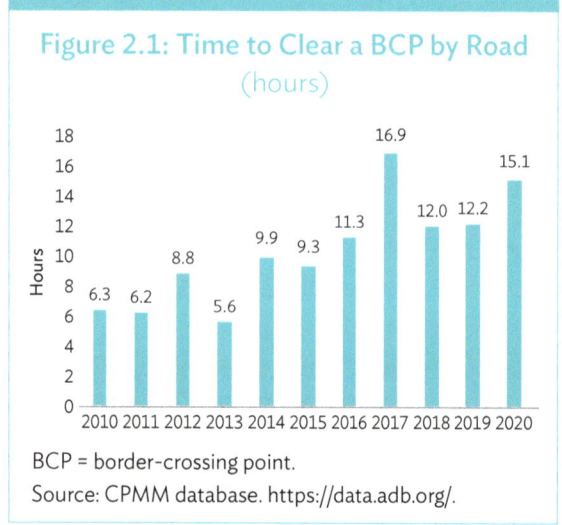

Figure 2.1: Time to Clear a BCP by Road (hours)

BCP = border-crossing point.
Source: CPMM database. https://data.adb.org/.

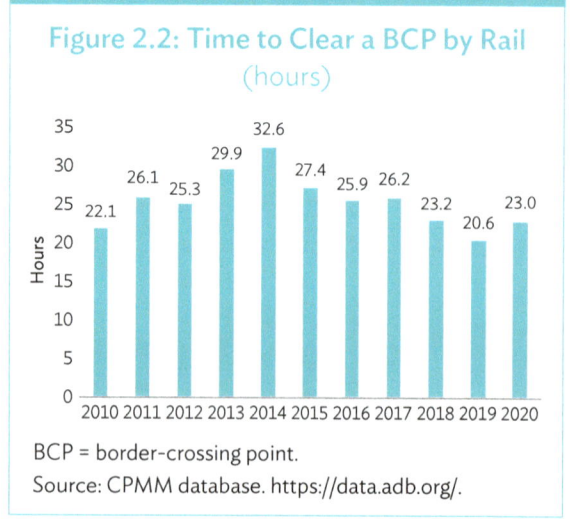

Figure 2.2: Time to Clear a BCP by Rail (hours)

BCP = border-crossing point.
Source: CPMM database. https://data.adb.org/.

Figure 2.3: Cost to Clear a BCP by Road ($)

BCP = border-crossing point.
Source: CPMM database. https://data.adb.org/.

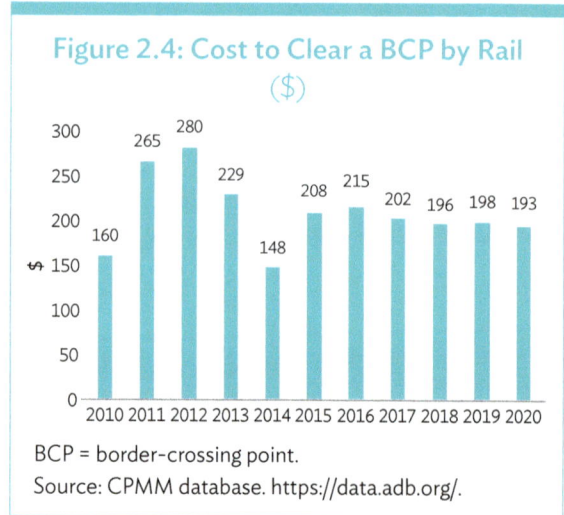

Figure 2.4: Cost to Clear a BCP by Rail ($)

BCP = border-crossing point.
Source: CPMM database. https://data.adb.org/.

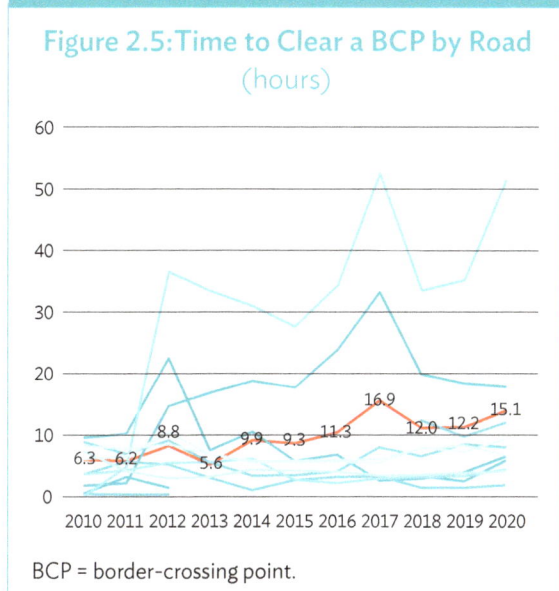

Figure 2.5: Time to Clear a BCP by Road
(hours)

BCP = border-crossing point.
Note: The red line depicts the regional average and the green lines indicate the 11 individual country information.
Source: CPMM database. https://data.adb.org/.

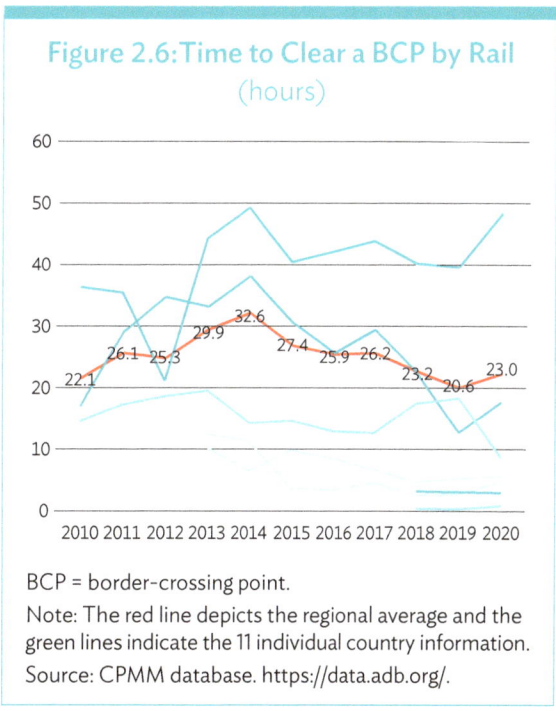

Figure 2.6: Time to Clear a BCP by Rail
(hours)

BCP = border-crossing point.
Note: The red line depicts the regional average and the green lines indicate the 11 individual country information.
Source: CPMM database. https://data.adb.org/.

that this has been gradually reduced since 2010 in the majority of CAREC countries. Further, the time in most countries is lower than the regional average. This indicates positive progress on border-crossing efficiency in most countries and lagging performance in a small number of countries. Therefore, reducing the more substantial border-crossing delays in the few countries that drive the regional average up can do much to improve overall regional performance.

This observation also applies to the average costs incurred to cross a border either by road (Figure 2.7) or by rail (Figure 2.8). Border-crossing costs in most countries are declining, but the persistent high costs in a few countries drive up the average costs. Notable factors for the improved efficiency across most countries include adoption of strong risk management measures, streamlining border control procedures, and greater data sharing among CAREC neighbors. National single windows and joint border cooperation also reduced time and cost at border crossings. Additionally, many countries are implementing digitalization of border processes to further reduce friction at the borders and promote trade. Appendix 1 provides details on the reasons behind this cross-country variation and looks at successful initiatives by individual CAREC members to improve trade facilitation at their borders.

To gain further insights on the changes over time, the CPMM nominal indicator for cost incurred at border clearance for road and rail transport was adjusted for inflation using the US consumer price index for all urban consumers (2010 = 100) and US gross domestic product (GDP) implicit price deflator (2010 = 100).[8] The unadjusted regional average cost incurred to cross a BCP by road (Figure 2.9) and by rail (Figure 2.10) show abrupt fluctuations. Upon adjusting for inflation, the resulting indicator has a

---

8   In the absence of a more suitable CAREC-wide indicator for deflation, the US Consumer Price Index and US GDP implicit price deflator are used as crude indicators to adjust the CPMM nominal cost indicators. In the original data, the consumer price index was set at 100 for 1982–1984 and the US GDP implicit price deflator was set at 100 for 2012. As the CPMM date started in 2010, these indicators are rebased to 2010 to demonstrate how CPMM real cost indicators fluctuate over time.

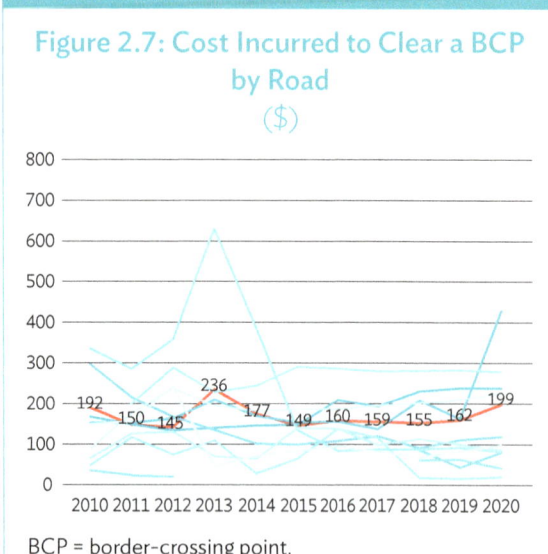

Figure 2.7: Cost Incurred to Clear a BCP by Road
($)

BCP = border-crossing point.
Note: The red line depicts the regional average and the green lines indicate the 11 individual country information.
Source: CPMM database. https://data.adb.org/.

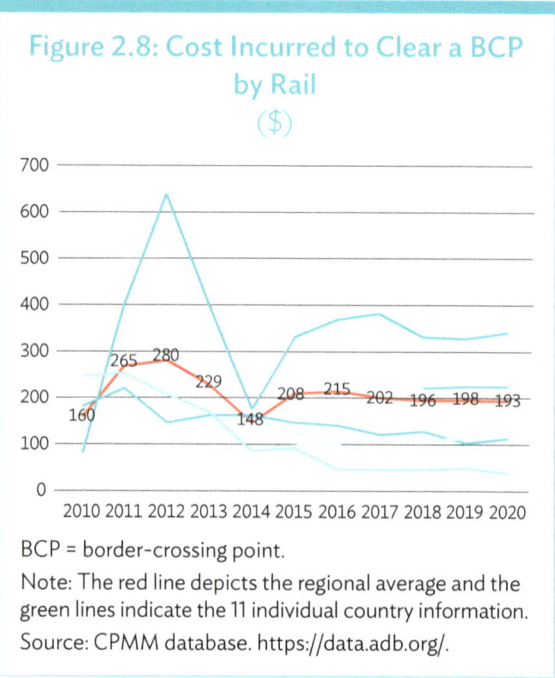

Figure 2.8: Cost Incurred to Clear a BCP by Rail
($)

BCP = border-crossing point.
Note: The red line depicts the regional average and the green lines indicate the 11 individual country information.
Source: CPMM database. https://data.adb.org/.

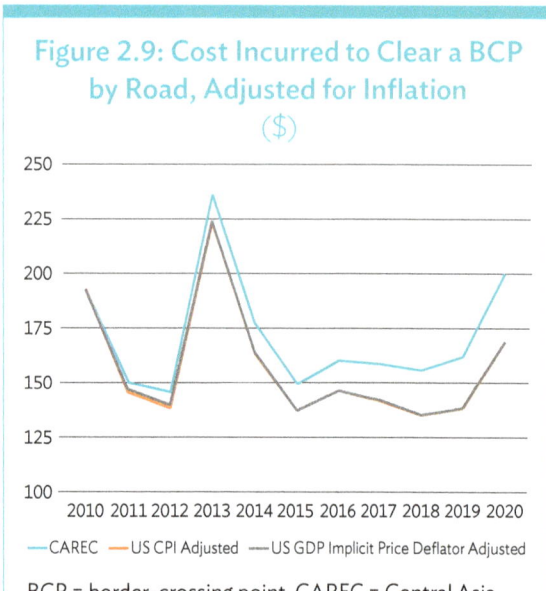

Figure 2.9: Cost Incurred to Clear a BCP by Road, Adjusted for Inflation
($)

— CAREC   — US CPI Adjusted   — US GDP Implicit Price Deflator Adjusted

BCP = border-crossing point, CAREC = Central Asia Regional Economic Cooperation, CPI = Consumer Price Index, GDP = gross domestic product, US = United States.
Note: The green line depicts Trade Facilitation Indicator 2 (TFI2) or the nominal regional average cost to cross a border. The orange and gray lines are the indicator adjusted for the US Consumer Price Index (2010 = 100) and US GDP Implicit Price Deflator (2010 = 100), respectively.
Source: Author's calculations; US Consumer Price Index and US GDP Implicite Price deflator were sourced from the US Federal Reserve Bank of St. Louis. https://research.stlouisfed.org/.

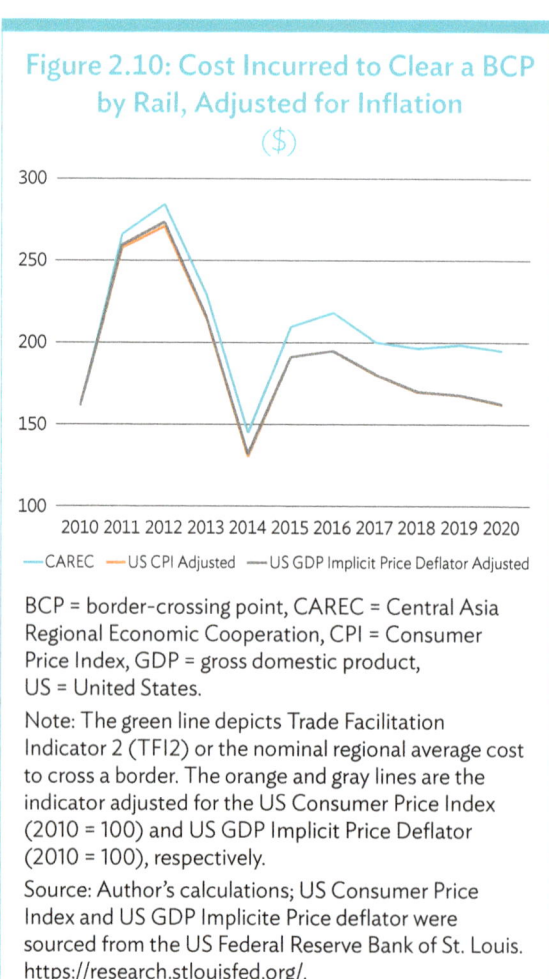

Figure 2.10: Cost Incurred to Clear a BCP by Rail, Adjusted for Inflation
($)

— CAREC   — US CPI Adjusted   — US GDP Implicite Price Deflator Adjusted

BCP = border-crossing point, CAREC = Central Asia Regional Economic Cooperation, CPI = Consumer Price Index, GDP = gross domestic product, US = United States.
Note: The green line depicts Trade Facilitation Indicator 2 (TFI2) or the nominal regional average cost to cross a border. The orange and gray lines are the indicator adjusted for the US Consumer Price Index (2010 = 100) and US GDP Implicit Price Deflator (2010 = 100), respectively.
Source: Author's calculations; US Consumer Price Index and US GDP Implicite Price deflator were sourced from the US Federal Reserve Bank of St. Louis. https://research.stlouisfed.org/.

slightly flatter trend, which indicates that the crossing costs at BCPs have remained relatively stable in real terms, especially since 2015.

The adjusted indicators further reveal a faster decline in real costs to cross borders by train, which has shown a downward trend since 2016. This demonstrates the increasing cost-efficiency in the rail transport. On the other hand, the real cost to cross borders by road exhibited a more erratic trend, albeit at a lower magnitude compared to the nominal cost.

Speeds

CPMM estimates that the speed without delay (SWOD) and speed with delay (SWD) of a truck are generally faster than a train (Figures 2.11 to 2.14).[9] This is because more stringent speed limits are imposed on trains to prevent derailing; also, trains face a longer border-crossing delay. A train must change gauge, and activities such as classification; waiting for priority trains to pass (e.g., carrying humanitarian aid supplies); and customs controls result in a longer border-crossing time.

A multipronged strategy is needed to improve speed. Connectivity between major cities, inter-cities, and urban–rural linkages would continue to require capital investment. Bridges, tunnels, and bypasses are required. Not only are highways needed but an emerging problem is also the urban congestion that affects freight movements. For example, truckers face challenges in cargo collection from Karachi port because access to the seaport is heavily congested. Institutional arrangements are also needed to streamline checks by traffic police, weight stations, and at BCPs. Protecting the local trucking

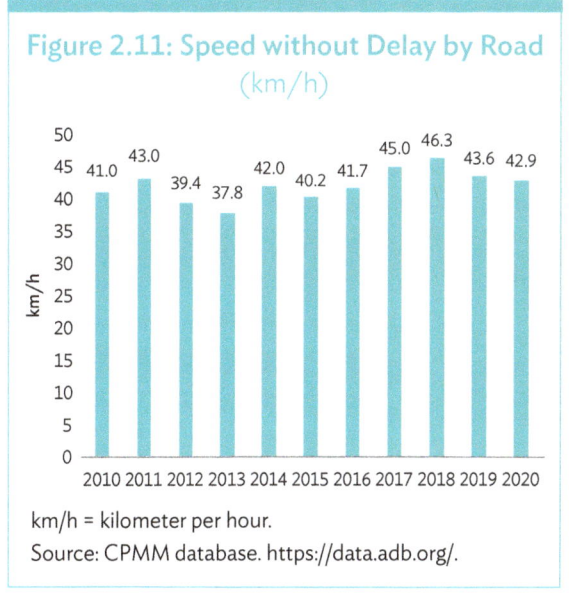

Figure 2.11: Speed without Delay by Road (km/h)

km/h = kilometer per hour.
Source: CPMM database. https://data.adb.org/.

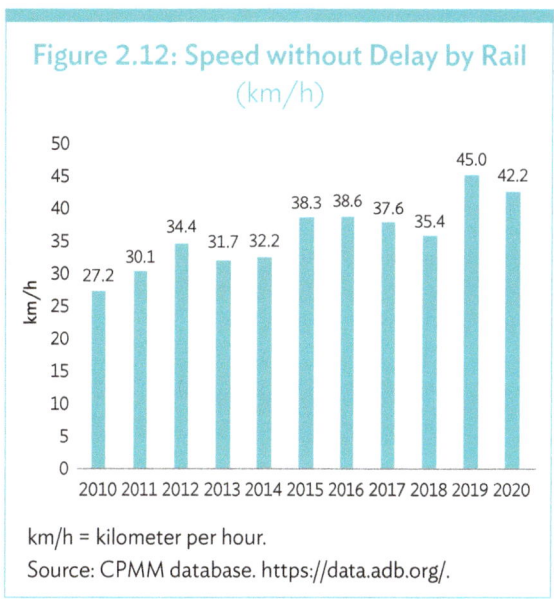

Figure 2.12: Speed without Delay by Rail (km/h)

km/h = kilometer per hour.
Source: CPMM database. https://data.adb.org/.

---

[9]   CPMM uses two measures of speed: speed without delay (SWOD) and speed with delay (SWD). SWOD is the ratio of the distance traveled to the time spent by a vehicle in motion between origin and destination (actual traveling time). SWD is the ratio of distance traveled to the total time spent on the journey, including the time the vehicle was in motion and the time it was stationary. Under CPMM, all activities considered as delay (customs controls, inspections, loading and unloading, and police checkpoints, among others) are recorded by drivers. SWOD represents a measure of the condition of physical infrastructure (such as roads and railways), while SWD is an indicator of the efficiency of BCPs along the corridors.

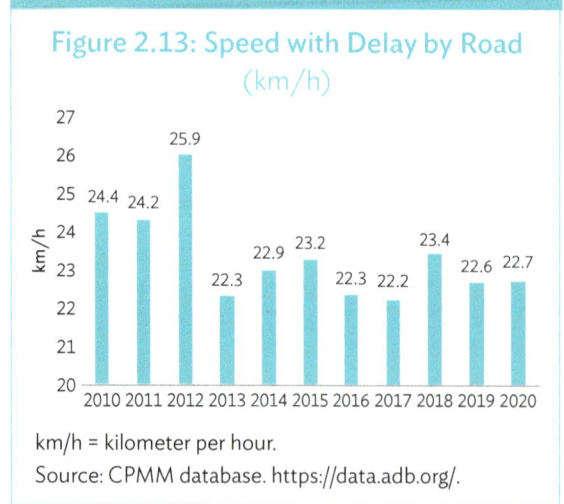

Figure 2.13: Speed with Delay by Road (km/h)

km/h = kilometer per hour.
Source: CPMM database. https://data.adb.org/.

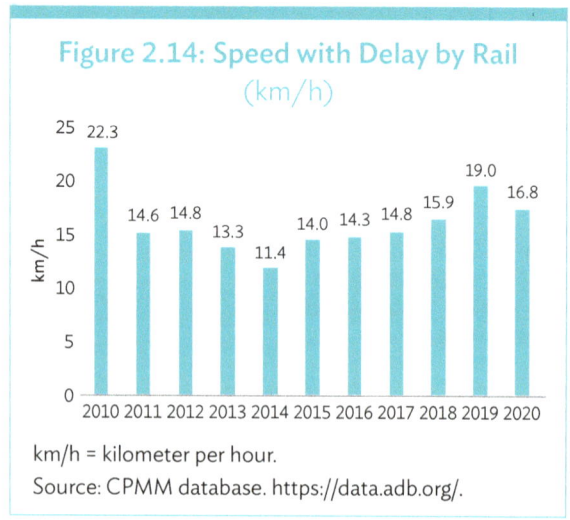

Figure 2.14: Speed with Delay by Rail (km/h)

km/h = kilometer per hour.
Source: CPMM database. https://data.adb.org/.

industry results in the erection of barriers in the name of noncompliance, resulting in the need for transloading at the borders. Addressing these issues would be highly beneficial to raise the average speed of shipment.

Trade Facilitation Progress

Much progress was made in CAREC trade and transport facilitation from 2010 to 2020. Customs and border management adopted more risk management measures, streamlining border control procedures, and strived toward greater data sharing among CAREC neighbors. National single windows were adopted or are under consideration. More CAREC countries entered into WTO agreements, such as Tajikistan (2 March 2013), Kazakhstan (30 November 2015), and Afghanistan (29 July 2016). Azerbaijan, Turkmenistan, and Uzbekistan became observers at the WTO. The container express train from East Asia to Europe was a significant development that shortened the economic distance, offering a transport mode much cheaper than air but much faster than sea. In 2011, the governments of Belarus, the PRC, Germany, Kazakhstan, Poland, and the Russian Federation signed an agreement to initiate that train service that permits the train to undergo an expedited service at the borders so that the overall transport time could be shortened. The train service offers a faster means (12 days) of connecting the markets in the Eurasian continent compared to the maritime route which takes 40 days, but more cost-effective than a direct air connection.

But impediments remain. The transit agreements, vehicle specifications, and sanitary and phytosanitary (SPS) standards have considerable differences between CARs and other regions. Drivers from four out of five CARs can freely cross borders of any other country from the regional group, but visa restrictions remain an issue and limit freedom of movement, since Turkmenistan requires a visa for the citizens from the other four CARs. Differences in axle load and vehicle dimensions require the transloading of goods from a foreign-registered truck to a locally registered truck at the border, raising transit time and costs.[10] Dissimilarities in the SPS and food safety standards result

---

[10] In general, the vehicle standards within the CARs and the Caucasus are more harmonized, but differ from standards in Afghanistan, the PRC, Mongolia, and Pakistan.

in rejection or delay of agricultural produce shipments, especially when such goods come from different subregions. Shipping documents, particularly for road freight, often result in the detention of goods due to missing or incorrect data created by language translation and valuation differences.[11] Regulatory and institutional barriers discouraging greater trade and integration exist. For example, differences in vehicle standards obstruct the trucks to enter and require transloading at the borders. Weight certificates that indicate the weight of the cargoes are not mutually recognized and trucks have to stop at weighing stations in transit countries to attain the certificate.

Growth of Container Express Trains

Initiated in 2011, the PRC–Europe express container train quickly became a significant contributor in boosting trade between the PRC and participating countries. Early express container trains connected with the Kazakhstan Temir Zholy at Alashankou–Dostyk (PRC–Kazakhstan). But after the completion of the Zhetygen–Altynkol railway, a new gateway opened up for PRC-Europe trains through the Khorgos-Altynkol BCP. This service has numerous advantages, including (i) shorter transit time (12 days compared to 45 days at sea), (ii) lower freight rate compared to air, (iii) ability to ship goods such as magnetic products normally prohibited by airlines, (iv) reduced pilferage compared to other conventional railways service due to shorter dwell time at railways stations, (v) more efficient customs clearance and documentation, and (vi) less corruption encountered as detaining such trains will attract higher levels of attention. Initially, the PRC government heavily subsidized to kick-start the service. With critical mass attained, driven by increasing load from Europe to the PRC (shipment of automobiles and parts and foodstuff), the PRC Ministry of Finance has mandated to stop all subsidies by the year 2021 and let market forces dictate the price of railways shipment. From 17 trains in 2011, the number had risen to 12,406 trains in 2020 (Figure 2.15).

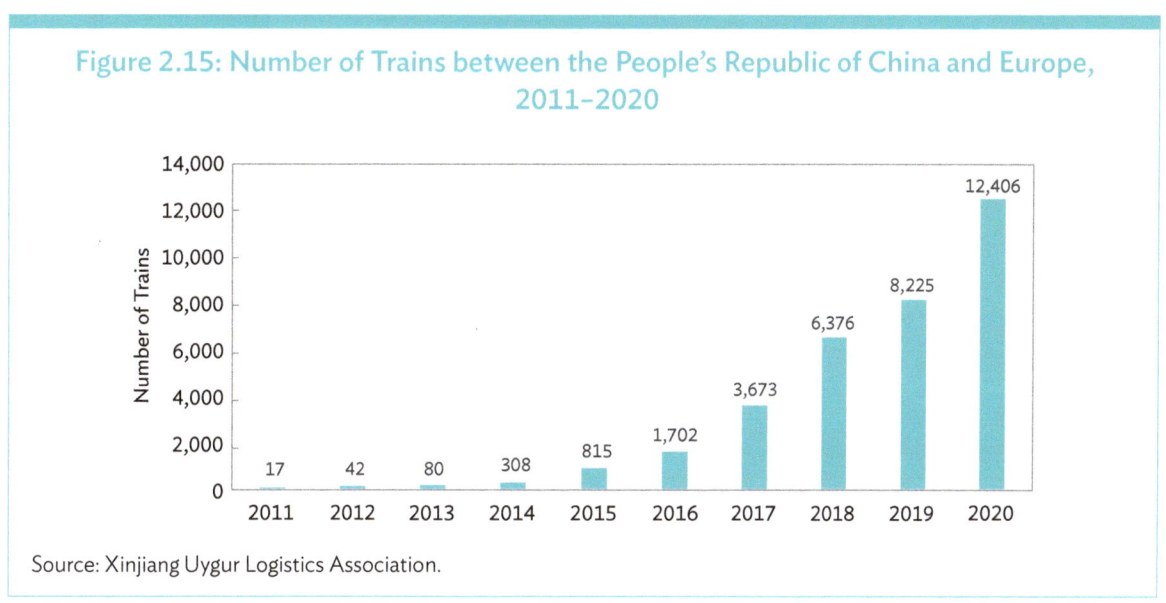

Figure 2.15: Number of Trains between the People's Republic of China and Europe, 2011–2020

Source: Xinjiang Uygur Logistics Association.

---

[11] Shippers declare the value of exports in commercial invoices, and the customs authorities at the destination have the right to assess if the valuation is reasonable. If not, the customs authorities will detain the goods and conduct further investigation. This is a particularly regular problem for East Asian or South Asian exports to CARs.

CPMM captures samples of express train time and cost data as they traverse the PRC and Kazakhstan routes. The faster speeds and shorter border crossing resulted in a faster 12-day turnaround of the train service. Within the PRC, trains registered an average speed of 62.5 kilometers per hour (km/h) in 2020, up from 11.7 km/h in 2010. This was largely attributed to express train shipments between Europe and the PRC. Similarly, speeds registered by trains traversing Kazakhstan jumped from 40.5 km/h in 2010 to 65.2 km/h in 2020.

COVID-19 Responses

CAREC conducted a comprehensive survey together with the CPMM partners in 2020 to understand the temporary measures imposed by each country and the associated impacts (Appendix 2).[12] CAREC member countries adopted strict measures at the beginning of the pandemic to contain the spread of COVID-19, which included various forms of border and sanitation controls such as

- imposing mandatory screening on drivers and transport workers crossing borders;
- designating sterile areas and quarantine zones;
- requiring personnel, vehicles, and shipments to undergo disinfection and sanitation measures; and
- closing BCPs completely and reopening them only gradually as conditions improved.

The controls were first imposed in March 2020, disrupting cross-border trade flows abruptly and significantly. CAREC countries instituted steps to support severely affected trade routes. These included a mix of relaxation of regulations, waiver of fees, and financial assistance. For instance, the PRC waived road toll fees in March 2020, resuming these on 6 May 2020. Kazakhstan introduced various measures to support small and medium-sized businesses, such as deferment of all taxes and social security contributions and postponing the submission date for tax filing from 31 March to 31 May 2020.

Still, border closures and movement restrictions[13] forced many truck drivers to stay home. As a result, operating costs surged, and business disruptions also forced some truck carriers to exit the industry. These led to a substantial drop in road transport capacity for both international and domestic shipments. Unsurprisingly, a significant percentage of cargo shipments were converted from road to rail. This is reflected in the traffic growth among most CAREC railways (including Azerbaijan,[14] the PRC, Kazakhstan,[15] the Kyrgyz Republic, Mongolia, and Uzbekistan[16]) during the first half of 2020. The rail

---

[12] These findings are also reported in the CPMM annual report for 2020. ADB. 2021. *CAREC Corridor Performance Measurement and Monitoring Annual Report 2020*. Manila.

[13] For example, Turkmenistan and Tajikistan closed their border to foreign trucks, while Kazakhstan and Uzbekistan required foreign truck drivers to present negative coronavirus certificates or pass COVID-19 tests at the BCP.

[14] In the first quarter of 2020, transit cargo via Azerbaijan increased by 32% year on year (Mincom.gov.az, 30 April). Between March and May 2020, about 140,000 tons of goods were transported via the Baku–Tbilisi–Kars Railroad, setting a new record (Apa.az, 17 June).

[15] Kazakhstan Railways (KTZ) reported 143 million tons of freight transported during the first 7 months of 2020, and a freight turnover of 131.6 billion ton-kilometers, which is 4% higher than the same period last year.

[16] During the first 5 months of 2020, rail transit cargo volume increased by 21%, export cargo volume by 14.3%, and import cargo volume by 0.4%, compared to the same period the previous year.

freight price increased in 2021, while the volume of goods transported on road also rebounded from 2020 as trade relations slowly normalized.

While most countries were emerging from the worst impacts of the pandemic in 2022, the COVID-19 outbreak and its devastating and widespread effects showed that all countries, including the CAREC Program members, need to strengthen their resilience and ability to manage trade flows when confronted with a crisis. Reflecting on the measures adopted during the pandemic and learning the lessons that it taught will put CAREC nations on a stronger footing when they must deal with future shocks. The pandemic once again highlighted the interconnectedness of the regions and the world's individual countries, and thus the great importance of regional cooperation and integration.

3 IMPEDIMENTS

Overview

CAREC countries are mostly landlocked. They exhibit several characteristics: (i) limited integration to global value chains; (ii) lower level of regional integration; (iii) narrow range of export commodities and trading partners; (iv) relatively low value-added processing, thus difficulty to move up the value chain; and (v) systematic impediments resulting in friction for cross-border movement of goods (Lee 2020).[17] This chapter analyzes key impediments in trade facilitation in the CAREC region.

Landlocked

Being landlocked is a major disadvantage in the contemporary world, where 90% of goods are transported using sea vessels (The Economist 2020). Among CAREC countries, only Pakistan and the PRC have seaports connected to the major maritime lanes. Azerbaijan, Georgia, Kazakhstan, and Turkmenistan have inland seaports due to the Black Sea and the Caspian Sea. Without a seaport, goods would have to be transported by land, such as roads and railways, invariably more expensive than water transport. Simply being landlocked would cut economic growth by about 0.5% (Sachs 2005), although this estimate would vary between resource-rich and resource-poor countries. The landlocked developing countries will not benefit from trade liberalization if a transit country obstructs access to international markets, further increasing the need for cooperation.

Access to international markets is important because many CAREC countries tend to produce similar products (due to similar climate and terrain), which leads to competition in similar exports. Imposing constraints to reduce transit traffic can thus become an effective way to limit the exports of competitors. The Almaty Programme of Action for landlocked developing countries in 2003 made key progress in offering a consistent set of policy actions. However, countries, especially Afghanistan and Tajikistan, are still subject to such transit obstructions. On the other hand, Georgia has traditionally facilitated transit, where many shipments (particularly machinery) are trucked across to Central Asia. After the liberalization of its transit regime, Uzbekistan has also increasingly gained importance as a transit nation.

---

[17] M. Lee. 2020. Five Keys to Expanding Central Asia's Global Value Chains. *Asian Development Blog*. 26 November. https://blogs. adb.org/blog/five-keys-to-expanding-central-asia-global-value-chains.

Constraints at the Seaports and Inland Waterways

The Convention on Transit Trade of Land-locked States obliges signatories to provide a corridor for transporting goods to and from seaports. Four seaports are relevant in CAREC (Table 3.1).

Table 3.1: Seaports in the CAREC Region

Localities	Seaports	CAREC Countries
Pacific Ocean	Lianyungang Tianjin	People's Republic of China
Indian Ocean	Karachi Gwadar	Pakistan
Caspian Sea	Baku Aktau Turkmenbashy	Azerbaijan Kazakhstan Turkmenistan
Black Sea	Poti, Batumi	Georgia

CAREC = Central Asia Regional Economic Cooperation.
Source: ADB. 2021. *Ports and Logistics Scoping Study in CAREC Countries.* Manila.

Despite the abovementioned convention, ground realities reflect multiple impediments within the seaports that affect landlocked countries' overall supply chain efficiency. For example, Tianjin is a gateway port for Mongolia, located 1,692 kilometers (km) from Ulaanbaatar. Port congestion means long dwell times at the seaports for inbound and outbound goods. The explosion at the Tianjin seaport in August 2015 disrupted the normal flow of goods to Mongolia. To mitigate the overreliance on Tianjin, Mongolia expressed interest in constructing a road–rail corridor to Jinzhou, another seaport in the PRC's northeastern region. Yet, Mongolia would require a huge investment to finance the railway infrastructure to Chifeng, a railway node connecting Jinzhou in the PRC.

Karachi is an all-weather seaport and could well serve as the gateway for landlocked Afghanistan and the CARs. Yet, the distance from the Karachi Port to Jalalabad in Afghanistan spans 1,509 km. The estimated time taken is 8 days, where 40%–50% is port dwell time, meaning a container does not move half of the time because it stays in Karachi due to customs procedures and other inspections.

The Trans-Caspian crossings harbor a different set of constraints. In principle, it offers a direct route that avoids the circuitous path going through the north of the Caspian Sea. However, adverse weather seriously delays the vessels' schedule, making the estimated departure and arrival times unpredictable. Transport operators complain about the high cost of the ferry crossing, in addition to the high fees associated with transit, insurance, and permits.

Studies have estimated that inland waterways transport costs only 10% of road transport and 25% of railway transport under similar payload and conditions. The CARs have inland waterways, but the infrastructure is underdeveloped. For example, river crossing at the Amu Darya between Afghanistan and Uzbekistan depends on the barge service, which is often unreliable. The Pakistan Indus River of 3,200 km has the potential of inland waterways transportation. However, there is little inland waterways infrastructure and fleet due to vested interest by the road transport sector, lack of investment, and shallow water draught at certain locations.

Economic Concentration on the Raw Materials Exports

The high concentration of export products and being landlocked of many CAREC countries confined export and underdeveloped value-added processing.[18] Thus, many CAREC countries are restricted to export raw materials with a low-value content, coupled with long-distance and border crossings, resulting in the dual challenge of transporting low-unit value commodities using a relatively costlier transport mode (road) (Coke-Hamilton 2019). The concentration of trade is particularly evident in Afghanistan, Azerbaijan, Mongolia, Tajikistan, and Turkmenistan (Table 3.2). For instance, 96% of Azerbaijan exports relied on hydrocarbons.

Table 3.2: Measuring Concentration in Trade for CAREC Countries, %

Countries	Partners		Products	
	2010	2019	2010	2019
Afghanistan	81	91	77	82
Azerbaijan	62	60	97	96
Georgia	56	21	62	61
Kazakhstan	55	52	90	86
Kyrgyz Republic	82	85	76	66
Mongolia	95	97	94	94
Pakistan	46	43	61	65
People's Republic of China	48	42	55	54
Tajikistan	79	81	78	85
Turkmenistan	71	91	91	98
Uzbekistan	82	75	74	74

CAREC = Central Asia Regional Economic Cooperation.
Note: Data for Tajikistan is from 2014 to 2019 and Uzbekistan is from 2017 to 2019.
Source: Consultant's analysis, based on extracted data from International Trade Centre Trade Map. https://www.trademap.org/Index.aspx.

The concentration level is examined by analyzing the merchandise export data from 2010 to 2019. The shares of the trade value by the top five export destinations ("partners") and the top five commodities categorized by two-digit HS code ("products") are compared. Four countries showed a high concentration (i.e., reliance) on both top five partners and products, where six countries showed a

---

[18] Economic concentration is not a trade facilitation impediment per se, but it poses challenges because when countries in the same region export similar products to similar export destinations, this invariably incentivizes transit countries to obstruct movement of competing products in their territory. In particular, the problem of such concentration has been widely discussed, such as in the World Economic Forum. https://www.weforum.org/agenda/2019/05/why-commodity-dependence-is-bad-news-for-all-of-us/ (accessed 14 September 2021).

high concentration in either partners or products. CARs traditionally export[19] to the Russian Federation due to the comparatively larger market size, more harmonized SPS, common language and practices, and insufficient food production in the Russian Federation. Yet, such a lack of diversification is risky because economic and geopolitical shocks could derail economic growth. The CARs experienced this in 2014 when economic sanctions against the Russian Federation and the collapse of oil prices led to currency devaluation and adverse impact on the CARs. Similar negative impact is expected in the near future as a result of the ongoing Russian invasion of Ukraine. Afghanistan also has a narrow base of exports, mainly agricultural products and carpets, and reliant on nearby markets such as India and Pakistan and less ability to export to farther markets. Azerbaijan export is exceedingly focused on hydrocarbons. Mongolia exports comprise mainly of minerals and hides, and have a high dependence on access to the Tianjin seaport in the PRC to connect to farther markets. Within the CAREC members, Georgia, Pakistan, and the PRC have a more diversified trade structure and the presence of seaports give these three countries an added advantage to maritime access to international markets.

On the other hand, concentration could also be an outcome of transit difficulties. Afghanistan continued to rely on India and Pakistan as its foreign markets for agricultural products (which accounted for two-thirds of its exports overall), but could not sell to other destinations such as Kazakhstan because Afghan transport operators could not obtain the road permits and visas needed for transit shipments through neighbor countries. Despite the reactivation of the Transports Internationaux Routiers (TIR) or International Road Transports Convention in 2013, Afghanistan transport operators, in general, could not use transit routes across Central Asia. Ad hoc border tensions between the Kyrgyz Republic and Tajikistan resulted in temporary border closures at times, thus requiring trucks to reroute.

Transit Challenges

Regional trade agreements were designed to resolve transit differences and produce a set of uniform rules and procedures so that goods could move rapidly across the CAREC region. Regional initiatives, such as the Cross-Border Transport Agreement (CBTA) and the Quadrilateral Traffic in Transit Agreement (QTTA), were launched in CAREC countries. Unfortunately, these efforts stalled. The CBTA, which involved Afghanistan, the Kyrgyz Republic, and Tajikistan, could not be operational as the Kyrgyz Republic disapproved the Karamyk BCP as an international BCP. The QTTA, which involved Kazakhstan, the Kyrgyz Republic, Pakistan, and the PRC, was not operational as Kazakhstan and the Kyrgyz Republic do not fully implement the condition of QTTA.

The TIR Convention 1975 continues to be the most widespread transit system used for cross-border road shipment. All CAREC countries were contracting parties, although TIR only started operations in Afghanistan (in 2013), Pakistan (in 2016), and the PRC (in 2018). By utilizing mutually agreed customs controls and exchanging shipment data, transport operators using TIR could be exempted from repeated customs guarantees and inspections in each transit country.

Yet, some CAREC countries have shown a decline in the number of TIR carnets. The main reason was the decision of the Russian Federal Customs Service to implement its own transit regime and restrict the

---

[19]   CARs export fresh fruits and vegetables, dried fruits and nuts, textiles, and apparels to the Russian Federation.

effectiveness of TIR through the Russian Federation. Since many CARs shipments were bound for the Russian Federation, this impacted CARs' decision to use TIR. The formation of the Eurasian Economic Union (EAEU) further reduced interest in using TIR in Kazakhstan and the Kyrgyz Republic for trade with the Russian Federation. TIR was also perceived to be costly, especially for shorter hauls. Approved TIR holders need to put in a security deposit to the TIR Association based on the number of approved trucks, which must be re-certified every 2 years. The implementation of TIR in Afghanistan, the PRC, and Pakistan showed the need to modify legislation, upgrade capacity building, and build an information infrastructure to achieve full effectiveness. As these conditions are still in progress in Afghanistan and Pakistan, TIR adoption has been slow in these countries. Even with TIR, border crossing could be refused due to the difficulty of obtaining road passes for vehicles and visa permits for drivers, areas the TIR convention does not cover.

CAREC member countries have expressed interest in developing a regional transit system that is simpler and more cost-effective than TIR for short hauls. CAREC has supported an initiative, the CAREC Advanced Transit System,[20] initially piloted between Azerbaijan, Georgia, and Kazakhstan. Any multilateral, regional transit system would need an insurance guarantee chain and the recognition of customs authorities to be successful.

In the absence of a multilateral agreement for transit, road permits and quotas are common. While the creation of the EAEU resulted in the removal of customs borders between Kazakhstan and the Kyrgyz Republic, the trading bloc erected some barriers for Tajikistan, Turkmenistan, and Uzbekistan. In addition, trucks from East Asia and South Asia could not traverse across CARs. This led to the need for the repeated transloading of goods between trucks.

COVID-19 caused another surge in border-crossing time as many BCPs imposed stricter measures to examine drivers and goods, pushing up the average border-crossing time and cost in 2020. Yallama and Saryasia, two BCPs at Uzbekistan, were the most time-consuming, and their strict epidemiologic controls and quarantine reflected similar measures taken by other BCPs in the region. As new mutations of COVID-19 emerged, there was also distrust of vaccine certificates from overseas sources. Thus, all foreign drivers entering Uzbekistan BCPs, for example, were required mandatory tests. The waiting time in the quarantine zone at the border for the test results extended the overall border-crossing time in 2020.

Border crossing for trains has fundamentally different characteristics. Unlike road transport, where the unit is a vehicle, a wagon or container in a train does not move independently. As a unit of shipment, rail freight depends on the movement of the entire train. Impediments could be attributed to infrastructure and regulatory barriers.

---

[20]   The CAREC Advance Transit System proposes the creation of a single harmonized electronic regional transit system among participating countries. It aims to streamline and harmonize existing transit documentations and promotes the development of a modern, risk-based affordable guarantee mechanism that rewards compliant economic operators.

First, differences in railway gauges between the former Soviet Union states and the other CAREC countries result in the breakage of tracks, necessitating the transfer of freight at the BCPs. The former Soviet Union states adopt the broad gauge (1,520 millimeters [mm]), the PRC uses the standard gauge (1,435 mm), whereas Pakistan utilizes 1,676 mm. Second, the availability of rolling stocks such as wagons is a constraint affecting the movement of trains. Missing wagons at the BCPs would hold up the border crossing. Third, regular freight trains cannot move if there are trains carrying priority shipments, such as foodstuff, energy, medical supplies, and disaster relief materials. Fourth, CARs and the PRC are members of the Organization for the Cooperation of Railways and use the Agreement on International Goods Transport by Rail (SMGS Agreement) consignment note for cross-border rail freight. Missing or erroneous data causes border-crossing delays. This happens when a railway station in the PRC issues a domestic consignment note. The information is then transferred into the SMGS consignment note at designated railway stations in the PRC before moving across the border, where translation or manual errors occur. Finally, the shortage of material-handling equipment hampers the railway's operations and contributes to border-crossing delays.

High Transport Cost

When different transport modes are evaluated, other things being equal, the most expensive mode is air, followed by road, rail, pipeline, and water. In CAREC, shipments tend to rely heavily on road and rail transport, which in many instances requires a change of railways gauge at the border. The use of inland waterways as a commercial means to transport goods is nearly nonexistent in many CAREC countries. Rivers in CAREC countries are sometimes deployed to generate hydroelectric power, so dams would imply that rivers could not be utilized for freight transport. For example, Pakistan's Indus River stretches from north to south, but is undeveloped for inland transport. The reliance on road transport, the underdeveloped transport infrastructure, and the low degree of more cost-effective transport modes, such as inland waterways, explain why the total transport cost estimate remains elevated over the years. However, road and rail transport costs receded from the peak in 2013–2014 (Figure 3.1 to 3.2).[21]

The cost estimate includes the carriage cost, border-crossing costs (TFI1), and informal payments.[22] The high transport cost is also compounded when items with low-value density,[23] including product categories such as raw agricultural produce, are shipped. These items with a low-value density cannot not bear the high cost of transport. This constraint limits market access of their produce because shipment over long distances would be prohibitively expensive. Table 3.3 on a comparison of shipping two products illustrates this challenge.

---

[21] The high cost coincided with the period when Kazakhstan acceded to the Eurasian Economic Union (EAEU), and the rails reformed in the country which actually increased, rather than decreased cost.

[22] The estimates are scaled to the cost of carrying 20 tons of goods over 500 km due to CPMM samples having varying origins, destinations, and payloads. Transport cost is derived from a myriad of many factors but primarily on distance and tonnage, which is why CPMM cost estimates are scaled as such.

[23] Value density is measured by the total product value (from commercial invoice) divided by the weight (kilogram). Simply put, it is the price per kilogram.

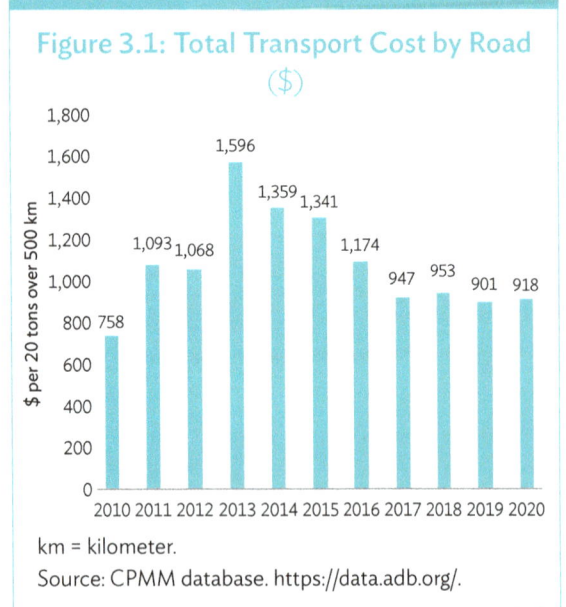

Figure 3.1: Total Transport Cost by Road ($)

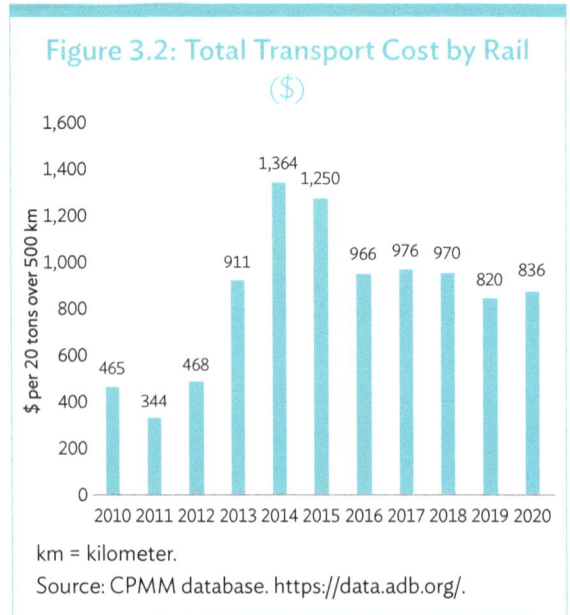

Figure 3.2: Total Transport Cost by Rail ($)

Table 3.3: Impact of High Transport Cost

Product	Apples	Pharmaceutical Drugs
Commercial value	$10,0000	$1,000,000
Tonnage	20,000 kg	20,000 kg
Unit price	$0.50/kg	$50/kg
Transport cost	$2,000	$2,000
Unit transport cost	$0.10/kg	$0.10/kg
Transport cost as % of commercial value	20%	0.2%

kg = kilogram.
Source: CPMM database. https://data.adb.org/.

Using the above hypothetical example, one could see that a shipper of apples must bear 20 cents (20%) for every $1 apple sold. In contrast, the shipper of pharmaceuticals needs to pay only 0.2%. A dual approach is required to address this problem. The first approach is to modernize the physical transport infrastructure to improve connectivity and efficiency of trade flows, thus reducing costs. The second is to encourage upward value migration of the products, such as processing raw materials instead of selling unprocessed items. The decompression of the transport cost as a percentage of the commercial value would benefit access to further export destinations.

Complex Documentary Requirements

Another well-documented impediment is the complexity of documentation. To import or export goods, traders need to complete multiple documentation and secure permits and approvals. While some countries, notably Azerbaijan and Georgia, have established a "one-stop-shop" service and others, such as Kazakhstan, have implemented recent solutions, others require traders to visit different ministries and agencies to complete the paperwork. Electronic systems are used selectively or are absent. Hand signatures are commonplace.

Table 3.4 illustrates the amount of effort to complete paperwork for export or import. Exporters in three countries (Afghanistan, Kazakhstan, and Mongolia) spent more than 100 hours to complete the paperwork for one shipment and spent $200 or more in five countries. Three countries (Afghanistan, Pakistan, and Tajikistan) require the completion of 13 documents. Leading economies typically need only a commercial invoice, a packing list, a bill of lading, and a customs declaration. On the import side, the values for import time and costs are even higher compared to exports.

Table 3.4: Documentation Complexity by CAREC Country

Economy	Overall		Rank		Export Documentation		Import Documentation	
	Rank	Trading across Borders	Time (hour)	Cost ($)	Number	Time (Hours)	Cost ($)	Number
Afghanistan	173	177	228	344	13	324	900	11
Azerbaijan	34	83	33	255	6	33	200	6
PRC	31	56	8	70	6	11	75	8
Georgia	7	45	2	0	4	2	189	5
Kazakhstan	25	105	128	200	5	6	0	3
Kyrgyz Republic	80	89	72	110	7	84	200	2
Mongolia	81	143	168	64	9	115	83	6
Pakistan	108	111	55	118	13	96	130	10
Tajikistan	106	141	66	330	13	126	200	11
Uzbekistan	69	152	96	292	9	150	242	7

CAREC = Central Asia Regional Economic Cooperation, PRC = People's Republic of China.
Source: World Bank. https://www.doingbusiness.org/en/data/exploreeconomies (accessed 13 August 2021).

Complex Border-Crossing Procedures

Generally, the BCPs in the CAREC region conduct control activities only. This means that border authorities perform gatekeeper functions, such as visual inspections of drivers, goods, and vehicles, and high-level documentary checks. If compliance is detected, the vehicles are released to an inland facility for customs clearance. More advanced functions, such as detailed valuation of goods or laboratory tests, are usually not done at the BCPs due to the lack of equipment and technical personnel. Figure 3.3 describes the typical steps under a standard border-crossing procedure.

Trucks queue outside the BCP and wait for their turn to enter. Upon entry, different border authorities, starting with border security officers, will conduct checks on the driver and vehicle. Then, SPS, immigration, and transport controls are conducted; customs officers are usually the final authority to complete the procedure. Customs is empowered by legislation to be the final gatekeeper and detain the shipment if any unsatisfactory matters arise from the controls, even if the problem may not be customs

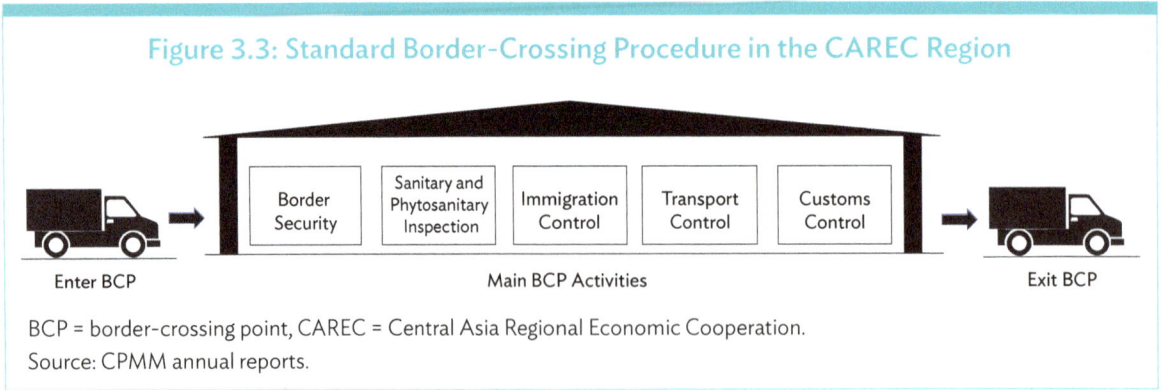

Figure 3.3: Standard Border-Crossing Procedure in the CAREC Region

| Border Security | Sanitary and Phytosanitary Inspection | Immigration Control | Transport Control | Customs Control |

Enter BCP   Main BCP Activities   Exit BCP

BCP = border-crossing point, CAREC = Central Asia Regional Economic Cooperation.
Source: CPMM annual reports.

related. For instance, a vehicle license problem or a driver's visa error could result in such detention. This sometimes results in an unfortunate situation where border-crossing delays are attributed to customs when the actual reason is beyond customs' areas of direct responsibility.

The need to complete border-crossing procedures and paperwork, often cumbersome, results in additional time equivalent to traveling a much farther distance. Due to this reason, shipment time and cost in Central Asia appear to be higher than the timings in other parts of the world, such as Europe, despite the apparent proximity.

Unharmonized Standards

Efficient cross-border trade requires that the documentary compliance and other border requirements (such as waybills, road permits, certificates and other forms related to SPS, and laboratory tests) of CAREC members become more standardized. The lack of such harmonized standards is a root cause of delays in cargo clearance and border crossing across the region. When CAREC members do not recognize one another's certifications, examinations and tests often need to be repeated.

Corruption

Rent-seeking behavior, such as exhorting fees above the legitimately published tariffs, amounts to corruption. In many instances, transport operators resort to such payments to obtain a favor, such as getting a permit, shortening the queuing time, getting early completion of clearance, or avoiding penalties due to overloaded goods. Some general observations on corrupt behavior are outlined as follows:

- Corrupt behavior can happen anywhere but is a high risk and very common at the BCPs due to the substantial costs that will be imposed on shippers and transport operators if a shipment cannot clear quickly.
- Corruption tends to be more prevalent at the BCPs with high traffic.
- Corruption tends to be less common in rail transport, as holding up a train is more difficult and demands a greater justification than holding back a truck.

At high-traffic BCPs, a Russian term *tolkach* is used to describe "pushers" or unofficial personnel designated by border authorities to "facilitate" paperwork needed to cross a border. Transport operators are sometimes referred to these *tolkach* to fill up the documents to avoid being refused entry or exit.

CPMM analyzed unofficial payments in the CAREC region every year (Table 3.5). For 2020, rent-seeking behaviors by likelihood of occurrence were (i) vehicle registration (48%), (ii) phytosanitary activities (28%), (iii) customs controls (24%), (iv) transport inspection (21%), and (v) weight and standard inspection (18%). Compared to 2011, the likelihood in encountering unofficial payments at the border grew for vehicle registration, phytosanitary activities, and customs control. However, substantial decline was seen in other activities. In terms of the magnitude of unofficial payment per truck, the largest sums were taken at escort or convoy ($102) and customs control ($79).

Table 3.5: Estimated Unofficial Fees per Activity (Road Transport), 2011 and 2020

Activity	2011		2020	
	Likelihood (%)	Average ($)	Likelihood (%)	Average ($)
Border Security and/or Control	26	20	1	4
Customs Controls	23	51	24	79
Commercial Inspection	–	–	1	7
Health and/or Quarantine	17	7	17	4
Phytosanitary	17	6	28	5
Veterinary Inspection	18	3	5	2
Visa and/or Immigration	43	7	6	3
Transit Conformity	–	–	1	5
GAI and/or Traffic Inspection	33	9	0	–
Police Checkpoint or Stop	30	10	0	–
Transport Inspection	21	9	21	5
Weight and/or Standard Inspection	21	14	18	6
Vehicle Registration	40	15	48	4
Emergency Repair	2	41	1	5
Escort or Convoy	0	6	1	102
Loading and Unloading	14	52	0	3
Road or Bridge Toll	24	15	1	3
Waiting or Queuing	2	8	0	–

– = data not available, GAI = Gosudarstvennya Avtomobilnaya Inspektsyya.
Source: CPMM Annual Report 2020.

Transport operators shared that corruption was lesser at the beginning of the pandemic when many border officers had to return home or work from home. This showed that reducing the number of human interventions could help curtail corruption. This could be achieved when digitalization and digital tools are adopted to automate processes.

4 CAREC SOLUTIONS

This chapter briefly reviews the efforts by CAREC countries and evaluates progress made, and the areas needing further attention.

Key Efforts on Transport and Trade Facilitation

In total, $41.1 billion was invested in 218 projects under the CAREC Program during 2001–2021. ADB provided $15.6 billion (38%) of the financing, while the rest are funded by various development partners and CAREC member country governments.[24] The transport sector received more than $30.0 billion (75%), followed by energy at $8.9 billion (22%), and trade at $1 billion (3%). Technical assistance under the program totaled nearly $679.13 million during the period.[25]

These projects developed infrastructure, equipment, and digitalization. They also supported process, capacity, and institution building. Transport sector investments accounted for 75% of the total and were largely dedicated to infrastructure operations. These projects rehabilitated roads, expanded railway capacity through the procurement of rolling stock and the electrification of tracks, and developed logistics centers. The institution building supported modernizing, harmonizing, and reforming legislation and regulations, and led to bilateral or multilateral agreements to facilitate cross-border trade.

Under CAREC, several investment projects were completed to rehabilitate roads, construct new roads to improve connectivity, and finance the rolling stocks and railways network.[26] Such efforts facilitated the gradual increase in speed without delay (SWOD) for road and rail shipments. CPMM estimation of road transport in Mongolia, using data before and after the road rehabilitation program was completed, provides evidence to demonstrate the effectiveness of the investment programs. Although both road and railways have achieved a SWOD over 40 km/h, this is still considered low compared to the average traveling speed in Europe, where a heavy-goods vehicle could move at 80 km/h.[27]

Did the transport road and rail infrastructure completed under the projects actually improve regional connectivity and integration? This is a complex question as myriad factors can affect the outcomes. Broad trade facilitation indicators shown in Figures 2.1 to 2.4 and 2.11 to 2.14 present a mixed picture

---

[24] CAREC Program website. https://www.carecprogram.org/.

[25] ADB. 2022. *CAREC 2030 Development Effectiveness Review (2017–2020)*. Manila.

[26] Some notable accomplishments have included the rehabilitation of the Bishkek–Osh Road; the Regional Road Development and Maintenance Project, Phases 1 and 2 in Mongolia (Altanbulag–Zamiin-Uud); and the Salang Tunnel project in Afghanistan.

[27] European Commission. *Mobility and Transport: Road Safety*. https://road-safety.transport.ec.europa.eu/eu-road-safety-policy/priorities/safe-road-use/safe-speed/archive/current-speed-limit-policies_en (accessed 7 September 2021).

for the region, but examination of the country-level indicators provides a clearer picture on which countries have performed better (Appendix 1).

For example, Mongolia benefited from the road rehabilitation program completed in 2014. The SWOD indicator increased from 24.2 km/h in 2013 to 33.4 km/h in 2014, and later reached 50.0 km/h. This improved performance was attributed to the paved road connecting Altanbulag and Zamiin–Uud. The PRC saw a steady reduction in border-crossing time, mainly due to the improvement at Khorgos. The launch of railway operations there at the end of 2012 provided an alternative to the Alashankou rail route. On the other hand, Kazakhstan, which received 22% of the CAREC-related investment, showed that despite the consistent improvement in the rail transport SWOD, which rose from 40.5 km/h in 2010 to 65.2 km/h in 2020, longer border-crossing delays were significant enough to slow the overall speed of the delivery of goods during the 2010–2020 period. This shows that continued attention is needed to both infrastructure that can improve connectivity through traffic congestion relief and the streamlining of border crossing procedures.

Operations such as the Regional Improvement of Border Services (RIBS) projects add value in this regard.[28] The RIBS in Pakistan, for example, focuses on upgrading the performance of the Torkham, Chaman, and Wagah BCPs and will be instrumental in improving the overall performance of CAREC Corridor 5. Corridor 5 has been perennially identified as the worst-performing CAREC corridor, and the average crossing time at Pakistan BCPs surged from 29.9 hours in 2015 to 55.7 hours in 2021. The long-standing issues at these BCPs were exacerbated by impacts of the COVID-19 pandemic. In view of the latest dialogue for trilateral cooperation by Afghanistan, Pakistan, and Uzbekistan to build Central Asia–South Asia connectivity, the RIBS effort appears timely.

While CAREC projects focus on road and rail transport, the attention paid to other modes is growing. The new CAREC Transport Strategy covers aviation, and the CAREC Program has supported the Aktau seaport's expansion during the past decade. The seaport provides an alternative east-west route between Central Asia and the Caucasus.

Other Efforts

Efforts were launched to modernize customs and adopt more risk-based management, as well as to harmonize SPS. This led to participation of Uzbekistan in the ePhyto Solution in October 2020 and the country has since processed around 15,000 certificates with European countries through the ePhyto Hub. Projects also covered the financing of equipment such as X-ray scanning machines to expedite vehicle inspections at BCPs. Capacity-building programs were implemented to enhance the organizational ability of CAREC policy makers and regulators—for example, by introducing customs officials to the best practices of modern trade procedures recommended by the World Customs Organization. They also provided a platform for dialogue and mutual understanding through the CAREC Customs Committee. Digitalization and process optimization projects involved reviews of

---

[28] Regional border services improvement projects coordinate infrastructure improvements and border-crossing clearance procedures in the Kyrgyz Republic, Mongolia, Pakistan, and Tajikistan. ADB. Regional: Central Asia Regional Economic Cooperation Regional Improvement of Border Services Project (Kyrgyz Republic and Tajikistan); ADB. Pakistan: Central Asia Regional Economic Cooperation Regional Improving Border Services Project; and ADB. Mongolia: Regional Improvement of Border Services.

existing workflows and the reengineering of steps to increase productivity, efficiency, and transparency. The CAREC Advanced Transit System pilot and support of eTIR efforts are works in progress.

The CAREC Program also focuses on developing economic corridors.[29] Among their many benefits are significant opportunities for expanding regional trade. The Almaty–Bishkek Economic Corridor and the Shymkent–Tashkent–Khujand Economic Corridor are currently under development, and new CAREC economic corridors could evolve. The possibilities include corridors between Mongolia and the PRC, and between Central Asia and South Asia, as well as a Trans-Caspian corridor connecting Central Asia and the Caucasus.

Financing under the CAREC Program has also gone into equipment to make cross-border freight movements more efficient. For example, one RIBS project component is providing equipment for a single-window system to cut processing time and costs at BCPs in the Kyrgyz Republic and Tajikistan. A new gantry scanner for the busy high-traffic Dautota BCP in Uzbekistan was also procured to expedite border crossing for freight vehicles.

Aside from providing hardware, the CAREC Program has conducted a series of workshops to build institutional capacity in customs, food safety, SPS, digital trade and e-commerce, transport, and technological innovation. The most recent activities promoted the use of digitalization to improve processes. One notable effort has been the creation of the Information Common Exchange to introduce a paperless trade system and the CAREC Advanced Transit System to provide a more effective way to manage transit shipments across the region. It is still too early to determine the impact of these initiatives, and continued support is needed for full implementation. The pandemic has provided impetus for the adoption of more digital tools, which would make economies more resilient during future supply chain shocks.

---

[29]   An economic corridor is a spatial concept. It defines a geographic region dedicated to or dominated by economic activities that may typically be focused on specific sectors such as information technology, production of specific manufactured commodities, tourism, etc. An economic corridor includes as prerequisites a good transport network; primary and secondary roads; and other infrastructure such as power, information and communication technology, and industrial parks. CAREC Program website. https://www.carecprogram.org/?page_id=18146.

OUTLOOK 5

The ongoing events, investments, and national and regional initiatives will reshape the flow of goods across the CAREC region and transform the existing corridors and practices. This chapter highlights some pertinent developments.

Increased Diversification and Emergence of New Economic Corridors

In recent years, CARs have increased their imports from the PRC and Europe substantially. For some of them, the volume of the PRC and European trade has exceeded trade with the Russian Federation. Further, the PRC has increased the import of agricultural products from Central Asian countries (e.g., Kazakh wheat and canola oil). In addition, consumer preference for safe, organic, tasty fruits and vegetables has spurred the purchase of more Central Asian produce (e.g., Uzbekistan's cherries). However, their road and rail networks were designed and built to connect with the Russian Federation. New economic corridors will likely emerge as CAREC members become increasingly integrated with global trade and diversify their markets.

Modal Shift to Rail

While improving post-pandemic in 2022, the coronavirus pandemic had sharply reduced the air carriage capacity as many passenger planes were grounded in 2020, and cross-border freight by road was subjected to temporary border closures and stringent controls. This problem had extended to ocean freight as shippers scrambled to ship their goods when the economies reopened and, as a result, bid up the ocean freight price. From August 2019 to August 2020, the price index for shipping a 40-foot container had risen from $1,500 to $10,000.

Since vessel capacity would unlikely increase in a short time, this high international ocean freight cost would continue in the near future, which paves the way for continuous shift to rail mode of transportation. In 2022, the ocean freight rate decreased after the Russian invasion of Ukraine started. This event disrupted normal traffic and, coupled with the aggressive tightening policy of the Federal Reserve, resulted in 'demand destruction' and lower demand for transportation. By October 2022, the Drewry World Container Index (this measured the average cost of sending a 40-foot ocean container between high traffic origin-destination) dropped to $3,688. Thus, the restrictions on road transport and the high ocean freight rate are expected to divert freight traffic to rail transport. This could lead to increased border-crossing time at railway terminals and an increased rail freight rate in 2022.

Digitalization

Industry 4.0 highlights the importance of machine-to-machine communication through sensors and smart devices to automate data transfer. Innovative solutions such as artificial intelligence, blockchain, and data analytics are being applied in transport and supply chain management and customs modernization, hence enhancing trade facilitation. For instance, smart seals that are compliant with customs technical specifications are being used in Asia and Africa to provide real-time track and trace while securing the integrity of the goods and improving border services.

Cross-Border E-commerce

E-commerce logistics has reshaped how items get into the buyers' hands. The concept of self-collection lockers, modern urban logistics, and e-fulfillment centers are used in developed countries for e-commerce logistics. This will also influence the developments in the CAREC region as an increasing number of consumers purchase items online and expect fast deliveries.

The latest CAREC Transport Strategy includes air transport as a strategy. In a post-pandemic environment, container freight trains and improved air connectivity cost-efficiency, could support the growth of e-commerce. Cross-border e-commerce has influenced a generation of new consumers and buying habits in the PRC partly due to the huge success of Alibaba and JD.com. Cross-border e-commerce will also impact logistics, tax, marketing, international express, and local deliveries.

The potential of e-commerce in the CAREC region is significant. User penetration in CAREC was only 21% in 2019 versus 41% globally, and the average revenue per user was 10 times lower than the global average (Table 5.1).[30] Both business-to-business and business-to-consumer e-commerce should be encouraged to facilitate trade. To do so, CAREC countries would need to standardize and harmonize the legislation in customs, taxation, intellectual property, insurance, rules of origin, and many other considerations to fulfill the potential of e-commerce. Postal services and private enterprises serving as e-commerce marketplaces, technology service providers, payment gateways and solutions, and last-mile logistics companies will likely reshape transportation and logistics.

Increased TIR Utilization

All 11 CAREC member countries are contracting parties to the 1975 TIR Convention. The pace of utilization will likely accelerate as both Pakistan and the PRC adopt TIR to send freight overland. In August 2021, the first shipment of mangoes was dispatched from Pakistan to the Russian Federation using TIR. The consignment left Pakistan at Taftan/Mirjawa (Iran) border for Moscow (Russian Federation) via the Tehran–Astara (Azerbaijan)–Astrakhan (Russian Federation) route. The road distance spans 4,600 km, and it took about 7 days (FBR 2021). Since acceding to the TIR Convention in 2016, the PRC has run several pilots and significantly increased the number

---

[30]   The estimations above removed the PRC to obtain a fairer picture because the PRC is advanced in e-commerce applications. It is not fair to lump the entire nation to the CAREC estimates.

Table 5.1: Use of E-commerce in CAREC Countries, 2019

Country	Number of Users (million)	User Penetration (% of population)	Average Revenue per User ($)
Afghanistan	n.a.	n.a.	n.a.
Azerbaijan	3.1	31	101.22
PRC	855.1	61	1,008.80
Georgia	1.3	35	78.03
Kazakhstan	7.0	38	129.26
Kyrgyz Republic	1.5	23	33.10
Mongolia	0.8	24	38.12
Pakistan	41.0	19	51.92
Tajikistan	1.4	15	21.60
Turkmenistan	0.9	15	21.50
Uzbekistan	8.5	25	42.32
CAREC-10	65.4	21	60.15
CAREC-11	920.5	54	941.42
World	3,170.8	41	607.07

CAREC = Central Asia Regional Economic Cooperation, n.a. = not applicable.
Note: CAREC-10 includes all CAREC countries except the People's Republic of China (PRC). CAREC-11 includes all CAREC countries. Data for Afghanistan is not available.
Source: ADB (2021).

of PRC–Europe cargoes carried by trucks under TIR carnets. By June 2019, all 13 BCPs in the PRC's Xinjiang Uygur Autonomous Region and all interior customs offices were designated as TIR offices. Consequently, European carriers have begun to target high-value shipments that require fast, reliable service between the PRC and Europe.

Managing Corruption

Over the past decade, the level of corruption has decreased in some areas, thanks to multilateral efforts to eradicate corruption via effective reforms (e.g., Georgia).[31] This could be further improved with the introduction of information and communication technology and risk adoption. The use of technology, such as online declarations, tends to reduce human "touch points" and makes collecting informal fees impossible. Adoption of risk-based management programs such as authorized economic operators (AEOs) and random sample inspections would reduce congestion and create a less compelling environment for transport operators to pay "tea money" to shorten the queuing time.

---

[31] World Bank. 2012. *Georgia's Fight Against Corruption in Public Services Wins Praise*. 13 January.

6 RECOMMENDATIONS AND CONCLUSIONS

The CAREC region occupies a strategic location in the Eurasian continent and could connect major economies as a land bridge. There are complementary areas within CAREC countries, such as the energy surplus in CARs and the energy deficit in South Asian members. Broad initiatives such as improving the investment climate, diversifying the product export portfolio, and enhancing regional connectivity in "hard" and "soft" infrastructure need to be implemented. If successful, the CAREC region can become an economically vibrant area, well integrated with the international trade lanes despite its physical constraints. Failing to do so would limit the countries' economic expansion; they would serve only as pure transit countries with little economic value added and mainly export raw materials in the form of agricultural produce or energy commodities. This chapter highlights specific transport, transit, and trade facilitation measures that could create a difference.

Expand Cross-Border Transport and Logistics Infrastructure

CPMM identified border crossing as a major impediment and long waiting time as a result when entering a BCP. A reason for the time-consuming delay at high-traffic BCPs is the underdeveloped infrastructure and layout, which affect throughput capacity. International donor organizations can support CAREC governments address the demand for public goods, such as constructing more and better-paved asphalt surface roads connecting the BCPs. At the same time, private investment and operators could be attracted to build revenue-generating facilities such as parking lots for heavy transport vehicles. The drivers can utilize roadside facilities such as banks, motels, cafés, and automobile repair centers. In addition, logistics centers and cross-docking stations could be constructed to temporarily store goods that need to be transloaded between trucks. Temperature-controlled storage is another useful service, considering the significant trade volume of perishable agricultural goods in the region.

Harmonize Transport and Vehicle Standards

Differences in transport and vehicle standards lead to the need for frequent transloading of trucks. Unless a foreign operator holds a bonded carriage license (which is very limited), the truck is typically not permitted to cross the border if it does not belong to the same "bloc."[32] This leads to the

---

[32] A bloc refers to the regional grouping. The former Soviet Union states in Central Asia and the Caucasus are considered as one. The PRC and Mongolia are considered East Asian. Afghanistan and Pakistan are considered South Asian. Typically transport operators from one bloc need to change vehicles at the border when they enter another bloc.

time-consuming and costly action of transferring freight from one truck to another. Although TIR is an effective solution, it cannot waive the need to transfer shipments because it does not exempt the need for vehicle passes. Another key concern is that nations can adopt protectionist measures to impose cabotage rules and protect the local trucking industry from foreign competition.

A solution is to comprehensively review all transport and vehicle standards and build a minimal standard for truck dimensions, axle loads, safety standards for vehicles and drivers, road signs, and navigation rules. A beneficial initiative is harmonizing the weight bridge certificate and avoiding repeated weight inspections en route. Modernizing the weight bridge stations is another key initiative, such as using digital weight bridges and minimizing the probability of corruption. Once this harmonization is in place, CAREC countries can consider increasing the road quotas for one another, raising the number of road permits, and improving the efficiency of cross-border shipment by road carriage.

Enhance Customs Efficiency and Transparency

CAREC countries have made some commendable progress, and the CAREC regional platform has facilitated discussions through the Customs Cooperation Committee. Further efforts directed at the national single window, joint customs cooperation, mutual exchange of trade data, and simplification of the declaration would be useful. The transition from a customs officer as a controller to a trade facilitator would require the appropriate tools, technologies, and legislation. Mutual learning from one another would also be helpful. For instance, other CAREC countries can learn from the customs clearance zones (CCZs) established in Georgia, supported by innovative designs, technologies, and practices, which helped expedite cross-border shipments.

Coordinate Border-Crossing Operations

Border-crossing operations refer to the types, sequence, and complexity of activities a shipment needs to complete at the BCPs. Customs, inspections, and documentary checks occur and assign the shipment to the green, yellow, or red channel. Coordinated border-crossing management involves (i) standardizing the border-crossing operating hours, (ii) extending the operating hours on both sides, (iii) establishing green lanes for TIR shipments and time-sensitive cargoes, (iv) facilitating advanced shipping notification or declaration that allow risk management, and (v) offering "one-stop-shop" service.

A highly efficient approach Is to adopt joint border management where a shipment crosses only one BCP instead of two (one entry and one exit) at the border. While this is not possible for air and seaport terminals, such a concept is possible for land BCPs. However, such an idea is complex, as sharing a common BCP may not sit well with policy makers or among border agencies. Yet, there is hope. Under joint customs control, Azerbaijan and Georgia are proposing a new BCP at Abreshumis Gza–Ipek Yolu. If successful, such an experiment may offer lessons for a more streamlined and efficient border crossing.

Authorized Economic Operator

The AEO is a special group of qualified entities that move goods across borders and enjoy privileges such as expedited clearance. These entities could be shippers or transport operators. Based on the World Customs Organization Standards to Secure and Facilitate Global Trade, the AEOs must meet strict criteria before being admitted. Once an entity becomes an AEO, it can enjoy a simplified border-crossing and customs clearance process. Pakistan launched a national AEO program in 2019, and Tajikistan did the same in 2020. Once the national AEO programs are established and fully operational, CAREC countries can consider a regional AEO system where the qualified entities between members are mutually recognized to magnify the benefits on a regional scale.

Container Freight Trains

Given that it is improbable to completely eradicate COVID-19 soon, border crossings would continue to require stringent inspections that introduce excessive delays and costs, particularly if the control measures are not designed, or the technologies are not in place to improve productivity. Container freight trains have started in recent years, transporting goods in containers from the PRC to different destinations in the CAREC region. Containers provide a secure means to move goods and alleviate the need to examine the goods physically. It is recommended that countries strengthen the infrastructure and adopt practices to facilitate container trade. For example, if the cranes are not available, moving containers in a container yard is impossible. By having such elements in place, goods could be moved quickly and efficiently between the production and consumption nodes in a supply chain.

Concluding Remarks

The CAREC region—with abundant hydrocarbon, mineral, and agricultural resources—has immense opportunities due to its strategic location at a time when interest in an overland corridor connecting Asia and Europe has become globally important. The COVID-19 pandemic has disrupted business and international trade in the CAREC countries, but also incentivized the development of new corridors and means of doing business. This has included a review of the value of using trains to ship goods across the region.

CAREC's opportunities in facilitating inter- and intra-regional trade come with risks and cannot be taken advantage of without overcoming obstacles. CPMM is an evaluation and monitoring tool to assess corridor efficiency, identify impediments, and inform the preparation and implementation of solutions. CPMM uses information collected by the private sector to accumulate the data from which it derives its findings every year. It was created primarily to enable policy makers to identify bottlenecks, determine the overall efficiency of corridors, and measure national performance in trade facilitation.

Throughout this publication, CPMM offers empirical evidence to describe developments, impediments, and accomplishments. There are plans under way to enhance the CPMM methodology and make it more robust. In addition, the project team is working with external partners—other aid agencies, donor organizations, think tanks, and academic institutions—to promote the use and application of the

CPMM methodology to a broader audience, including policy makers, private sector operators, policy research institutions, and academe.

Some general insights can be distilled from this publication and the four main trade facilitation indicators it has covered. The average time to cross the border by road gradually increased, which suggests that road transit across the CAREC region still needs to improve. One prime reason is the difficulty of using the same truck to carry a shipment the entire route from its origin to its destination. Trucks from the former Soviet Union states can move across their borders with ease, but those from East Asia and South Asia do not have this privilege. This requires the transfer of the freight a foreign truck is carrying to a locally registered one and increases the time and costs of border crossings.

The average border-crossing cost and the total transport cost have been declining in most CAREC countries (i.e., they have become more cost-competitive). But the region is likely to face increased shipping costs because COVID-19 has increased the cost of doing business. Governments have offered waivers, rebates, and other measures to cushion the impact of the pandemic, but these are temporary. Because elevated ocean freight rates have diverted shipments to alternative transport modes such as rail, increased demand is projected to raise rail freight rates as well.[33]

In the longer term, more cost-effective freight transport modes, such as the use of inland waterways, could be considered as the CAREC countries tend to rely primarily on road and rail. Progress has been observed in increasing the speed of both road and rail transport, as well as inland waterways. This is testimony to the improved connectivity established by the various investment programs completed in this decade. Still, the average traveling speed of a vehicle at 42 km/h could be raised further. Heavy transport vehicles attain speeds up to 80 km/h in Europe. This would require a well-connected transport infrastructure network and a minimal amount of stopping during transit for police checkpoints, weight stations, and emergency repairs.

It is also heartening to witness the closer collaboration fostered between CAREC countries over the past decade. This has been evident in border cooperation, sharing of data and information, participation in regional agreements, and standardization. Concluding trade agreements and ensuring no rollbacks in their implementation involve many complex considerations and require political will. The institutional or man-made barriers to smooth trade flow in the CAREC region can sometimes be more significant than the geographical or other natural factors. Border-crossing complexities, frequent physical examinations, and environments caused delayed clearance so that informal payments could be extracted, seriously impeding cross-border trade instead of facilitating it. CPMM is ultimately a tool used to measure corridor performance, but it is action by policy makers and all stakeholders that will be instrumental to driving improved trade facilitation.

This report provides insights into the relevant regional developments and impediments and offers recommendations. A key message is that institutional and policy barriers exist, but can be addressed through regional cooperation and integration. Implementing the necessary measures, such as proposed AEOs, requires political will. Through its CAREC Program, ADB remains committed to sustainable economic and trade developments in the region through greater cooperation and integration.

---

[33] This has reference to CPMM Annual Report 2020.

APPENDIX 1
COUNTRY PERFORMANCE

This appendix presents key developments and progress in trade facilitation in all Central Asia Regional Economic Cooperation (CAREC) member countries.

Afghanistan

Afghanistan[1] is strategically located at the crossroad between Central Asia and South Asia. However, security conditions and political instability limit its transit potential. The CAREC Corridors 2, 3, 5, and 6 traverse Afghanistan and its neighboring countries Pakistan, Tajikistan, Turkmenistan, and Uzbekistan.

Afghanistan's road network density is only 4 kilometers (km) per 1,000 square kilometers (km²), and only 52% of households are within 2 km of a road. About 7% of the roads are paved and more than 70% of interprovincial and inter-district roads remain in a poor state due to lack of maintenance and the rapid wear and tear from overladen traffic. The national ring road connects major cities (Kabul, Kandahar, Herat, and Mazar-e-Sharif) and integrates the four CAREC corridors. The Asian Development Bank (ADB) financed the road construction and road rehabilitation for 233 km of the national ring road, including the sections between Kabul–Jalalabad, Kabul–Kandahar, and Qaisar–Dari Bum. The World Bank rehabilitated the Salang Tunnel, a critical path for northbound traffic from Kabul to Central Asia. This is very beneficial because past Corridor Performance Measurement and Monitoring (CPMM) samples indicated that the Salang Tunnel became a bottleneck when heavy snow closed it. Drivers had to wait until the tunnel reopened, incurring high expenses and long waiting times. So, the rehabilitation of the Salang Tunnel contributed to the gradual lowering of total transport costs of the Trade Facilitation Indicator 3 (TFI3).

Since Afghanistan trade is import heavy, Corridor 5 plays an essential role—imports arrive at the Karachi seaport and are trucked to Afghanistan. Road transport is the only viable mode because the railways in Pakistan serve passengers predominantly. At the same time, despite the presence of the Indus River and smaller canals, inland waterways are not utilized to transport cargoes. A new development is the approval of the Gwadar for Afghan Transit Trade, which permits containerized cargoes to route through Gwadar and head to Afghanistan using Pakistan-bonded carriers. Another progress is Ghulam Khan's designation as the third international border-crossing point (BCP) (after Torkham and Chaman) to facilitate cross-border trade. However, key problems occur at seaports (port congestion and delay in

---

[1] This report is funded under ADB technical assistance that supports regular monitoring of the CAREC corridors and BCPs in Afghanistan. As the international community continues to assess the evolving situation in Afghanistan, ADB maintains the hold it placed on its assistance to the country effective 15 August 2021. This report was prepared based on information available as of 31 July 2021.

the release of goods) and at land BCPs such as Torkham and Spin Buldak (lack of proper parking space, disorganized queuing process, and rampant corruption).

Despite the intervention on infrastructure, policy and regulation barriers exist that prevent Afghanistan from realizing the potential to become a transit hub. The main reason is the stalled Afghanistan–Pakistan Transit Trade Agreement (APTTA) 2010. Both sides complained about noncompliance to conditions, such as transit rights. Thus, the trucks stop at the border and have to transload to other foreign-registered vehicles. Afghanistan trucks could not go beyond Peshawar to the Karachi seaport or Port Qasim. Pakistan trucks terminate at the zero lines at the Torkham border. In addition, unilateral ad hoc border closures disrupted border crossing and often resulted in long queues of trucks on both sides of the BCP. An example was the temporary closure of the Afghanistan–Pakistan border in the first quarter of 2017, which caused the average border-crossing time trend to spike. The joint implementation of a "24 by 7" operation at Torkham in September 2019 did the opposite by swiftly relieving the usual truck congestion. By the end of 2020, some positive signs emerged as policy makers from Kabul and Islamabad intensified their negotiations to renew the APTTA.

Table A1.1 shows the country-level CPMM trade facilitation indicators for Afghanistan from 2010–2020 for road and rail transport.[2] Between 2010 and 2020, the average border-crossing time at Afghanistan border deteriorated from 1.9 hours to 19.5 hours. Even longer delays which averaged 36 hours in 2017 were experienced by drivers particularly at Torkham and Spin Buldak borders with Pakistan due to temporary closure of the BCPs. In terms of cost, fees to cross a border

Table A1.1: Afghanistan—Trade Facilitation Indicators, 2010–2020

TFI	Road Transport	2010	2011	2012	2013	2014	2015	2016	2017	2018	2019	2020
TFI1	Time taken to clear a border-crossing point (hour)	1.9	2.3	15.8	18.2	20.4	19.2	25.8	36.0	21.5	19.9	19.5
	Outbound	*1.2*	*1.5*	*2.2*	*2.3*	*1.1*	*1.5*	*19.1*	*28.4*	*13.6*	*13.4*	*12.9*
	Inbound	*2.6*	*3.0*	*23.5*	*25.9*	*27.7*	*26.1*	*28.4*	*40.8*	*25.8*	*23.8*	*23.7*
TFI2	Cost incurred at border-crossing clearance ($)	169	151	137	143	149	152	212	196	233	240	240
	Outbound	*141*	*130*	*84*	*82*	*89*	*95*	*124*	*181*	*231*	*246*	*256*
	Inbound	*196*	*168*	*167*	*173*	*172*	*174*	*246*	*206*	*233*	*237*	*230*
TFI3	Cost incurred to travel a corridor section ($ per 500 km, per 20-ton cargo)	455	830	1,182	1,309	1,378	1,336	1,341	1,374	1,107	1,106	1,002
TFI4	Speed to travel on CAREC corridors (km/h)	24.9	24.7	12.5	16.4	16.8	16.2	13.6	13.9	12.4	12.3	12.4
SWOD	Speed without delay (km/h)	32.4	32.1	39.7	36.4	36.6	35.1	34.7	34.3	33.1	32.5	33.7

continued on next page

---

2   CPMM does not capture enough data on rail in Afghanistan to provide sufficient information on the trends.

Table A1.1   *continued*

TFI	Rail Transport	2010	2011	2012	2013	2014	2015	2016	2017	2018	2019	2020
TFI1	Time taken to clear a border-crossing point (hour)	–	–	–	–	–	–	29.7	–	4.1	3.8	3.8
	Outbound	–	–	–	–	–	–	*29.7*	–	*4.1*	*3.8*	*3.8*
	Inbound	–	–	–	–	–	–	*–*	–	*1.0*	*–*	*–*
TFI2	Cost incurred at border-crossing clearance ($)	–	–	–	–	–	–	299	–	222	225	225
	Outbound	–	–	–	–	–	–	*299*	–	*220*	*225*	*225*
	Inbound	–	–	–	–	–	–	*–*	–	*370*	*–*	*–*
TFI3	Cost incurred to travel a corridor section ($ per 500 km, per 20-ton cargo)	–	–	–	–	–	–	4,613	–	–	–	–
TFI4	Speed to travel on CAREC corridors (km/h)	–	–	–	–	–	–	2.5	–	–	–	–
SWOD	Speed to travel on CAREC corridors (km/h)	–	–	–	–	–	–	10.5	–	–	–	–

–= data not available, CAREC = Central Asia Regional Economic Cooperation, km = kilometer, SWOD = speed without delay, TFI = trade facilitation indicator.
Source: CPMM database (unpublished).

rose from $169 in 2010 to $240 in 2020. Similarly, cost incurred to travel a corridor section within Afghanistan rose from $455 in 2010 reaching a high value of $1,378 in 2014, before gradually declining to $1,002 in 2020. Transport speed of trucks (speed without delay [SWOD]) grew slightly from 32.4 kilometers per hour (km/h) in 2010 to 33.7 km/h in 2020. However, long border-crossing delays reduced shipment speed to speed with delay (SWD) of 12.4 km/h, which is among the lowest in the region. By 2020, border-crossing remained time-consuming as security in Afghanistan presented a prime concern, which increased the cost of shipment, as well as unofficial fees imposed on shippers and transport operators.

Azerbaijan

Azerbaijan is strategically located on the trade routes between Asia, the Middle East, and Europe. With Georgia and its ports on the Black Sea, Azerbaijan is part of a land bridge connecting the Caspian Sea with the Black Sea (and the Mediterranean Sea). In addition, Corridor 2 passes through Azerbaijan and shares a common border with another CAREC member, Georgia.

Azerbaijan has instituted several trade facilitation measures. These include using non-intrusive customs control systems, implementing "green channels," developing risk management and authorized economic operators (AEOs), embracing the e-customs concept and "single-window" system, and simplifying customs clearance of transit shipments.

CPMM studied the Trans-Caspian traffic and identified the Baku International Sea Trade Port in Alyat (new seaport location 70 km south of Baku) as an important gateway for transit traffic between the Black Sea region and Central Asia. Interestingly, the freight traffic in Baku increased in 2020 despite the challenges of the coronavirus disease (COVID-19) pandemic. The freight tonnage handled rose by 20%, and the number of twenty-foot equivalent units (TEUs) increased by 15% between 2019 and 2020. Early during the pandemic, the port authorities swiftly determined to keep the seaport operational. They instituted control measures to manage the risks of cross-border movement of freight and logistics workers.

One phenomenon of the water crossing was the long port dwell time at Baku. This is because the Caspian region's unpredictable weather patterns can change quickly in 45 days of a year. This could compel departing vessels to remain in the harbor and delay their departure for a few days. Other than that, the seaport is well equipped to handle additional traffic, with a capacity designed to handle 15 million tons and 100,000 TEUs annually. Based on the actual freight handled in 2020, the existing utilization accounted for 32% and 40%, respectively, for freight and container throughput.

At present, the governments of Azerbaijan and Georgia are negotiating the establishment of a joint international BCP "Abreshumis Gza" to facilitate the movement of passengers, vehicles, and freight. This project has the support of ADB and is officially listed in the CAREC Integrated Trade Agenda 2030. In principle, the joint conduct of customs procedures at this new node will streamline border-crossing operations, eliminate duplicate controls and inspections, and raise the productivity of staff and resources. This could lead to shorter time and lower costs at the new border point.

Some private transport operators complained about the high cost of water crossing at the Caspian. Thus, they resorted to a full overland route north of Kazakhstan, crossing the Russian Federation at the Kurmangazy BCP and entering Georgia at Lars BCP. This longer route added approximately 450 km of physical distance. The current ferry prices are estimated to be 40% below the market rate to compete effectively. The Azerbaijan Caspian Shipping Closed Joint Stock Company implemented this discounted strategy with the support of the Azerbaijan government, which understands the importance of positioning Azerbaijan as the logistics hub in the region.

At present, from Azerbaijan to Kazakhstan, the ferry ticket price for Kuryk–Alyat costs $900; Alyat–Kuryk, $1,200; and the Alyat–Kuryk–Alyat round trip costs $1,800. Between Azerbaijan and Turkmenistan, Alyat to Turkmenbashy costs $1,073 in either direction, and Alyat–Turkmenbashy–Alyat costs $1,716. The competitiveness of the fare could increase given that the Trans-Caspian International Transport Route is working on a through-fare rate for multimodal shipment (e.g., water–rail).

CPMM currently does not cover railway transportation in Azerbaijan, although the developments are monitored. The Baku–Tbilisi–Kars railway, once completed, will connect Azerbaijan and Georgia with Türkiye and the European rail network beyond. The Azerbaijan Railways (ADY), the state-owned railway, is an important economic actor. It transports critical oil equipment and supplies from Poti and Batumi to the Caspian Sea oil fields and returns with petroleum products. Over time, its freight traffic mix will be influenced by trade flow, modal shift, changes in freight characteristics, and user preferences. ADB and the World Bank support ADY in upgrading its network and improving its management effectiveness.

Table A1.2 shows Azerbaijan's country-level CPMM trade facilitation indicators for road transport during 2010–2020. The sparse data available indicated that[3] border-crossing time (6.3 hours) and cost ($85) in Azerbaijan were low in 2020 compared with the rest of the CAREC countries. This was the product of the efficient trade facilitation measures the country has instituted, including adoption of the e-customs concept and single-window systems. Trucks traversing the corridors within Azerbaijan registered a high average speed of 52.7 km/h (or 34.2 km/h accounting for delays at the border) in 2020.

Table A1.2: Azerbaijan—Trade Facilitation Indicators, 2010–2020

TFI	Road Transport	2010	2011	2012	2013	2014	2015	2016	2017	2018	2019	2020
TFI1	Time taken to clear a border-crossing point (hour)	0.5	3.3	1.5	–	–	50.7	–	–	3.6	2.7	6.3
	Outbound	*0.5*	*2.1*	*1.5*	*–*	*–*	*50.7*	*–*	*–*	*4.4*	*1.9*	*2.8*
	Inbound	*–*	*13.8*	*1.7*	*–*	*–*	*–*	*–*	*–*	*3.3*	*3.6*	*10.2*
TFI2	Cost incurred at border-crossing clearance ($)	–	30	27	–	–	710	–	–	91	50	85
	Outbound	*–*	*30*	*27*	*–*	*–*	*710*	*–*	*–*	*79*	*34*	*71*
	Inbound	*–*	*30*	*30*	*–*	*–*	*–*	*–*	*–*	*94*	*57*	*97*
TFI3	Cost incurred to travel a corridor section ($ per 500 km, per 20-ton cargo)	32	600	600	–	–	–	–	–	369	23	45
TFI4	Speed to travel on CAREC corridors (km/h)	16.0	36.9	35.6	–	–	–	–	–	30.2	34.0	34.2
SWOD	Speed without delay (km/h)	17.6	46.6	46.3	–	–	–	–	–	53.1	55.7	52.7

– = data not available, CAREC = Central Asia Regional Economic Cooperation, km = kilometer, SWOD = speed without delay, TFI = trade facilitation indicator.

Source: CPMM database (unpublished).

People's Republic of China

CAREC Corridors 1, 2, 4, and 5 pass through the People's Republic of China (PRC), which shares borders with Afghanistan, Kazakhstan, the Kyrgyz Republic, Mongolia, Pakistan, and Tajikistan. The PRC plays a critical role in CAREC trade. With its gross domestic product (GDP) expanding at a compound annual growth rate of over 10% from 2010 to 2019, it is a rich trade source for raw materials and finished goods. The country is a major importer of crude oil from Kazakhstan, natural gas from Turkmenistan and Uzbekistan, and developed the pipeline infrastructure to connect the PRC's Xinjiang Uygur Autonomous Region with these countries. It is also the largest buyer of coking coal from

---

[3] CPMM does not have an active freight forwarder partner in Azerbaijan tasked to collect shipment data. This limits CPMM's capacity to effectively measure trade facilitation indicators in the country.

Mongolian mines. In addition, the PRC is becoming the leading exporter of manufactured goods to most CAREC countries.

The PRC has focused on developing railways in its last three 5-year plans, strongly emphasizing containerization. The quality and coverage of China Railway's[4] network is indeed world-class and contribute substantially to facilitating trade and transport with CAREC countries. Cross-border rail growth had been substantial in 2020. According to China Railway, 2,158 PRC–Europe freight trains passed through Inner Mongolia Autonomous Region's Erenhot BCP in the first 11 months of 2020, increasing by 53.4% year on year. During the period, outbound trains were up by 54.3% to 1,023, and inbound trains were up by 52.6% to 1,135. To better meet the growth of the PRC–Europe freight train service, Erenhot rail station transformed part of its bulk cargo yard into container transloading for cross-border trains, increasing the handling capacity by around 30%.

The PRC is active in CAREC trade facilitation, improving its customs administration, collaborating with other CAREC members, and sharing good practices, including training border management officials from other countries. Over the past decade, notable progress and collaboration included the following initiatives:

Customs Reform

The PRC's focus gradually shifted from trade control to trade facilitation. The implementation of the single window, e-customs, process simplification, and the merger of the General Administration of Quality Supervision, Inspection and Quarantine into Customs are concrete examples.

Customs Cooperation

The PRC is making good progress in cooperating with CAREC member countries. On 1 November 2015, it started to exchange cargo manifests electronically with Mongolia's Customs at Erenhot and Zamiin-Uud and mutually recognized weight certificates and X-ray pictures. These led to a very substantial reduction of border-crossing times at the Zamiin-Uud/Erenhot road BCP.

"Go West" Western Development Policy

The Western Development Policy covers the western and interior regions of the PRC. This region contains 71.4% of the PRC's area but only 28.8% of its population.

The reform and opening up in the 1980s and 1990s benefited the coastal areas, especially the Pearl River Delta and the Yangtze River Delta, but left the PRC's interior underdeveloped. In an effort to reduce regional disparities, this policy aims to accelerate the economic development of Chongqing (a municipality directly under the supervision of the central government), Gansu, Guizhou, Qinghai, Shaanxi, Sichuan, Yunnan, Guangxi, Ningxia, Tibet Autonomous Region, and CAREC participants Inner Mongolia Autonomous Region and Xinjiang Uygur Autonomous Region.

---

[4]   China Railway is the trade name for China State Railway Group Company, Ltd.

Key features include infrastructure development (highways, railways, inland waterways, airports, river ports, and inland dry ports) and the relocation of modern industries. As a result, products manufactured in the western and interior regions are substantially cheaper (and faster) to ship to CAREC member countries, helping them be more competitive in CAREC markets. This policy is also tied to the Belt and Road Initiative and other important regional plans to form a unified national market and build a higher value-added economy. The annual National People's Congress in May 2020 affirmed this policy by announcing a new "Go West" plan.

Some achievements in trade facilitation include[5]

- streamlining trade processes, e.g., export and import permit applications;
- simplifying customs declaration, inspection, e.g., single window, one-stop processing;
- reducing government bureaucracy, like merging the General Administration of Quality Supervision, Inspection and Quarantine with Customs;
- digitizing to speed up trade, e.g., e-customs, government trade, and transport portals;
- acceding to regional trade agreements;
- spearheading customs cooperation with other CAREC members (e.g., data sharing with Mongolia's Customs);
- participating in Transports Internationaux Routiers (TIR) or International Road Transports Convention;
- generously subsidizing a significant number of trade goods; and
- promoting containerization and fast, reliable rail service.

Improvements in hard infrastructure include

- increasing the length and quality of highways, especially those leading to the BCPs;
- extending rail connection to most BCPs (even for the low volume Bichigt/Zuun–Khatavch BCP on CAREC Corridor 4c);
- enhancing rail track quality and signaling system for higher train velocity and larger payloads;
- expanding the throughput capacity and handling speed of many BCPs, e.g., Khorgos, Zamiin-Uud;
- developing many modern logistics centers, multimodal terminals, and inland dry ports; and
- creating special economic zones, especially at or near BCPs and inland dry ports along CAREC corridors (some are well equipped for handling cross-border e-commerce parcels).

Khorgos, located at the border between the PRC and Kazakhstan, is a gateway for goods between the two countries and serves road, rail, and pipeline traffic. Positioned as a transport and logistics hub, this BCP facilitates the following:

- International Centre for Border Cooperation, a 528-hectare bonded zone that contains wholesale trade centers for Central Asian buyers to conveniently visit and procure instead of traveling to further cities (Guangzhou, Yiwu, or Shanghai) for their business purchases.[6]

---

5   Belt and Road Initiative. 2017. https://www.beltandroad.gov.hk/index.html.

6   CAREC Program. International Center of Boundary Corporation - Khorgos. https://www.carecprogram.org/uploads/011_102_209_International-Center-for-Boundary-Cooperation-Khorgos.pdf.

- Khorgos Eastern Gate, a special economic zone that has warehouses and connected by roads and railways, serving as one of the largest "dry port" in the region to enable rapid movement and clearance of cross-border goods.
- Zhetygen–Khorgos railways line and Altynkol station became fully operational in December 2012 to serve freight by rail, on top of the freight by road.

CPMM data showed that the border-crossing time at Khorgos has dropped over the past decade. This duration has steadily shortened, a testament to improved infrastructure. Nonetheless, the total time and cost to transport a shipment from Urumqi and Almaty (approximately 1,000 km apart) remain elevated due to the need to change trucks at the border and the costly road section from Khorgos BCP to Almaty.

Table A1.3 shows the 2010–2020 country CPMM trade facilitation indicators for the PRC for road and rail transport. For road transport, average crossing time at the PRC borders declined to 7.1 hours from 10.2 hours over the period. However, CPMM has captured long delays at a few border-crossing points for outbound shipments. Takeshikent reported the longest duration (31.8 hours), followed by Horgos (16.4 hours). Meanwhile, border-crossing cost surged during 2010–2020 from $156 to $424. The costs incurred to travel through a corridor also grew from $532 in 2010 to $1,710 in 2020. Fees spiked at Horgos in particular and stood at $1,658 in 2020 due to the need during the pandemic to screen drivers, cargo, and material-handling equipment. This drove total transport costs up. Truck speeds in the PRC stood at 82.0 km/h in 2020, doubling the 41.0 km/h indicated in 2010. Speed with delay (SWD) averaged 47.2 km/h, the highest among CAREC countries.

Table A1.3: People's Republic of China—Trade Facilitation Indicators, 2010–2020

TFI	Road Transport	2010	2011	2012	2013	2014	2015	2016	2017	2018	2019	2020
TFI1	Time taken to clear a border-crossing point (hour)	10.2	11.0	24.2	8.1	11.4	6.3	7.3	2.9	3.1	4.3	7.1
	Outbound	*10.7*	*11.5*	*29.2*	*8.7*	*14.5*	*7.8*	*9.1*	*3.4*	*3.5*	*5.5*	*9.5*
	Inbound	*9.4*	*9.3*	*11.8*	*6.9*	*2.9*	*1.3*	*1.0*	*1.7*	*2.0*	*1.2*	*1.5*
TFI2	Cost incurred at border-crossing clearance ($)	156	155	165	212	172	156	159	141	211	166	424
	Outbound	*171*	*176*	*208*	*273*	*191*	*159*	*171*	*150*	*241*	*181*	*544*
	Inbound	*43*	*79*	*82*	*91*	*122*	*149*	*117*	*121*	*141*	*133*	*157*
TFI3	Cost incurred to travel a corridor section ($ per 500 km, per 20-ton cargo)	532	1,122	1,511	2,480	2,016	2,125	1,718	833	1,357	1,257	1,710
TFI4	Speed to travel on CAREC corridors (km/h)	21.7	21.0	15.4	12.9	16.0	16.6	15.3	23.0	22.0	25.9	47.2
SWOD	Speed without delay (km/h)	41.0	47.2	45.0	37.4	41.2	43.2	47.0	54.7	53.7	69.8	82.0

continued on next page

Table A1.3   *continued*

TFI	Rail Transport	2010	2011	2012	2013	2014	2015	2016	2017	2018	2019	2020
TFI1	Time taken to clear a border-crossing point (hour)	17.6	29.6	35.1	33.6	38.5	31.0	26.1	29.9	22.9	13.4	18.3
	Outbound	*17.2*	*21.9*	*30.6*	*35.4*	*35.7*	*26.9*	*16.3*	*22.0*	*14.8*	*11.9*	*18.7*
	Inbound	*23.5*	*44.5*	*40.2*	*29.6*	*44.9*	*39.1*	*44.4*	*41.8*	*45.8*	*17.7*	*17.5*
TFI2	Cost incurred at border-crossing clearance ($)	181	223	149	164	165	149	140	122	129	104	115
	Outbound	*209*	*286*	*166*	*155*	*128*	*91*	*80*	*78*	*68*	*33*	*24*
	Inbound	*84*	*144*	*140*	*173*	*216*	*221*	*240*	*199*	*202*	*128*	*150*
TFI3	Cost incurred to travel a corridor section ($ per 500 km, per 20-ton cargo)	639	664	873	1,346	1,731	1,612	1,031	808	976	789	678
TFI4	Speed to travel on CAREC corridors (km/h)	10.3	9.8	7.2	11.5	10.6	10.5	13.7	13.6	15.9	20.9	16.8
SWOD	Speed to travel on CAREC corridors (km/h)	11.7	16.4	25.7	41.8	47.5	22.9	55.2	56.2	50.2	65.1	62.5

CAREC = Central Asia Regional Economic Cooperation, km = kilometer, SWOD = speed without delay, TFI = trade facilitation indicator.
Source: CPMM database (unpublished).

For rail transport, trains took an average of 18.3 hours to cross the PRC borders in 2020. This was lower than the CAREC average (23.0 hours) and largely attributable to the marshaling of some trains to allow priority trains to pass. This indicator fluctuated over the period from a low of 17.6 hours in 2010 to a high of 38.5 hours in 2014. Long delays were reported at such rail BCPs as Alashankou, Erenhot, and Horgos. The situation is more serious at Alashankou, where the average delay was estimated at 26.9 hours in 2020. Train speeds within the PRC were fast and averaged 62.5 km/h in 2020—more than five times the 11.7 km/h speed in 2010. This was largely due to the high speeds of express train shipments between Europe and the PRC. Nonetheless, long border-crossing delays resulting from stringent pandemic-related sanitary controls greatly reduced the shipment speed along the CAREC corridors to 16.8 km/h in 2020 from 20.9 km/h in 2019.

Georgia

Georgia is the most recent member of CAREC, formally joining in October 2016. The border with Azerbaijan is the only one that belongs to another CAREC member country. CAREC Corridor 2 links Europe and Central Asia through the Caucasus. The significance of Georgia's membership in CAREC is immense because, for the first time, CAREC corridors can cover cross-border shipment from Lianyungang in the east, to the Caspian Sea, and then to Georgian seaports Batumi and Poti in the west. From these seaports, shipments can enter Europe through Istanbul in Türkiye, Varna in Bulgaria, or Odessa in Ukraine. Georgia is also one of the countries covered by the Lapis Lazuli corridor.

Georgia's successful customs and trade facilitation reforms have won worldwide acclaim and could be valuable lessons for other CAREC members.

The road network in Georgia spans over 20,000 km of roads. The existing infrastructure can support 8,000 motor vehicles daily and a maximum of 50,000 motor vehicles per day on automobile highways. The East–West Highway from Tsiteli Khidi–Tbilisi–Poti is the main corridor connecting Azerbaijan to the ports along the Black Sea. A truck takes approximately 7 hours to complete this east–west direction. The maximum permissible truck dimension is 4 meters (m) (height), 2.55 m (width), and 12 m (length). The load limit is 44 tons.

Supporting an annual capacity of 28 million tons of freight movements is 2,083.9 km of railways tracks. Georgian Railway is the national railway operator and a joint stock company, the only agency mandated to oversee the development of railway transport. Railways handle a substantial amount of transit cargoes (almost 60%).

Road and rail traffic displayed divergent patterns in the past few years. The decrease in freight by railways was the unfavorable economic environment that depressed demand for rail and the transfer of oil and energy products to newly completed pipelines. As a result, the private sector opined that the railway was losing competitiveness to road transport.

Georgia has taken effective measures to reform the customs and tax administration, and rankings of the World Bank's Doing Business reflected the success of those reforms. The Georgia Revenue Service (GRS) now integrates customs and tax into one administration, similar to the reorganization in Kazakhstan, where both functions are integrated into the Kazakhstan Revenue Committee. The GRS oversees customs procedures, sanitary and phytosanitary (SPS) border quarantine, veterinary border quarantine, and passport control for drivers at the borders.

On 1 January 2007, the Customs Code entered into force with dual objectives. First, the GRS aims to modernize customs practices and procedures to address previous deficiencies, where unclear rules on customs controls exist. Second, the GRS uses the Customs Code to detect corrupt behavior vigorously and impose penalties. A complementary effort involves upgrading the ASYCUDA World, which replaced ASYCUDA++ in 2015, and modernizing it into the latest version of "e-Customs.'" Technological innovation is instrumental in implementing risk-based management, which increases the number of vehicles in the green channel and lowers the chances of corruption.

Georgia also addressed trade facilitation by simplifying the organization of agencies at the border. Previously, many ministries and agencies were involved in the transport, transit, and trade regimes. The presence of multiple entities at the border—Customs Department (under the Ministry of Finance), Border Police (under the Ministry of Internal Affairs), SPS (under the Ministry of Agriculture), Transport Administration (under the Ministry of Transport)—complicated border crossings. Now, only two agencies are present: the GRS and Patrol Police.

The establishment of customs clearance zones (CCZs) is yet another significant reform. The CCZs are a single facility located near the BCPs and strategic locations to offer rapid customs documentation and clearance. The CCZs shorten cargo clearance time for cross-border trade. The steps and duration for border-crossing in the past were:

- Border security (15–30 minutes).
- Warehouse (1–2 hours).
- Broker for declaration (45 minutes to 1 hour).
- Commercial bank for payment (30 minutes to 1 hour).
- Cargo clearance (10–30 minutes).
- Examination (for red channel) (2–3 days).

At present, shippers visit a CCZ and use the e-Customs, where all cargo clearance is completed within 30 minutes or less. Clearance of shipments under the red channel extends for another few hours, compared to a few days in the past. Georgian legislation also guarantees that cargo transit is duty-free, and no customs guarantee, nor bond is required.

Georgia's seaports at Poti and Batumi are key gateways for transit traffic from and to Central Asia. The goods move between those seaports and Central Asian republics (CARs) over the Caspian Sea. The future establishment by Georgia and Azerbaijan of a joint international BCP, "Abreshumis Gza," to facilitate the movement of passengers, vehicles, and freight between the two countries is expected to improve transit efficiency. However, some structural challenges remain along this route. Other Caspian seaports have less capacity than Georgia's. Poti port can handle 550,000 TEUs annually, Baku's only 100,000 TEUs. The combined capacity of Aktau and Kuryk is 130,000 TEUs. In addition, while Georgian operators are prohibited from moving shipments overland through the Russian Federation, crossing the Caspian is more time-consuming and costly than using the now-banned overland route. A third challenge involves the added complication of meeting the different road, sea, and rail documentary requirements that multimodal transport presents. Communications between carriers and the consignees have not always been timely, especially regarding changes in original declarations on shipping documents. This results in complete or erroneous information.

Table A1.4 shows the country-level CPMM road transport trade facilitation indicators for Georgia during 2018–2020. The data demonstrated the relative efficiency of the country's transport and logistics, which was manifested in 2020 by a short average border-crossing time (13 hours), low border fees ($48), and low transport costs ($87). These results indicate that Georgia's trade facilitation measures, such as the CCZ, have been effective.

Table A1.4: Georgia—Trade Facilitation Indicators, 2010–2020

TFI	Road Transport	2010	2011	2012	2013	2014	2015	2016	2017	2018	2019	2020
TFI1	Time taken to clear a border-crossing point (hour)	–	–	–	–	–	–	–	–	13.4	10.6	13.0
	Outbound	–	–	–	–	–	–	–	–	*17.9*	*12.9*	*14.2*
	Inbound	–	–	–	–	–	–	–	–	*8.1*	*2.6*	*4.8*
TFI2	Cost incurred at border-crossing clearance ($)	–	–	–	–	–	–	–	–	66	68	48
	Outbound	–	–	–	–	–	–	–	–	*67*	*69*	*45*
	Inbound	–	–	–	–	–	–	–	–	*64*	*49*	*78*
TFI3	Cost incurred to travel a corridor section ($ per 500 km, per 20-ton cargo)	–	–	–	–	–	–	–	–	244	185	87
TFI4	Speed to travel on CAREC corridors (km/h)	–	–	–	–	–	–	–	–	18.8	21.5	27.1
SWOD	Speed without delay (km/h)	–	–	–	–	–	–	–	–	49.3	56.8	46.3

CAREC = Central Asia Regional Economic Cooperation, km = kilometer, SWOD = speed without delay, TFI = trade facilitation indicator.
Source: CPMM database (unpublished).

Kazakhstan

As the largest landlocked country in the world, Kazakhstan has immense transit potential. CAREC Corridors 1, 2, 3, and 6 traverse the country. The land BCPs serving road and railways are top ranking in terms of freight tonnage. Kazakhstan shares common borders with four CAREC members—the Kyrgyz Republic, the PRC, Turkmenistan, Uzbekistan—and the Russian Federation. Kazakhstan is a founding member of the Eurasian Economic Union (EAEU). The country has 96,245 km of roads[7] and facilitates several transit corridors. Shipments from the PRC to Central Asia pass through Khorgos and enter Uzbekistan and Turkmenistan to the west. The Kyrgyz Republic and Uzbekistan use Corridors 3 and 6 to access Russian markets in the north.

Khorgos is being modernized rapidly due to the investment by the PRC and Kazakh governments and private investors. The International Centre for Border Cooperation and the Special Economic Zone Khorgos Eastern Gate are the key beneficiaries with new terminals, logistics parks, and equipment to handle transit traffic (Figure A1.1). A large 129-hectare dry port handled more than 158,200 TEUs in 2019, up 16% from 2018. A notable improvement is the shortening of average border-crossing time at Khorgos. It dropped from 16.0 hours in 2010 to 5.7 hours in 2019.

---

[7]　Government of Kazakhstan. Bureau of National Statistics. https://stat.gov.kz/official/industry/18/statistic/7 (accessed 13 August 2021).

Nur Zholy is a new checkpoint for road traffic at Khorgos (Figure A1.2). According to the monitoring by the Nur Zholy state program, the average border-crossing time was reduced from 3 hours to 40 minutes.

Figure A1.1: A Yard Crane at Khorgos Eastern Gate Handling Containers on Rail

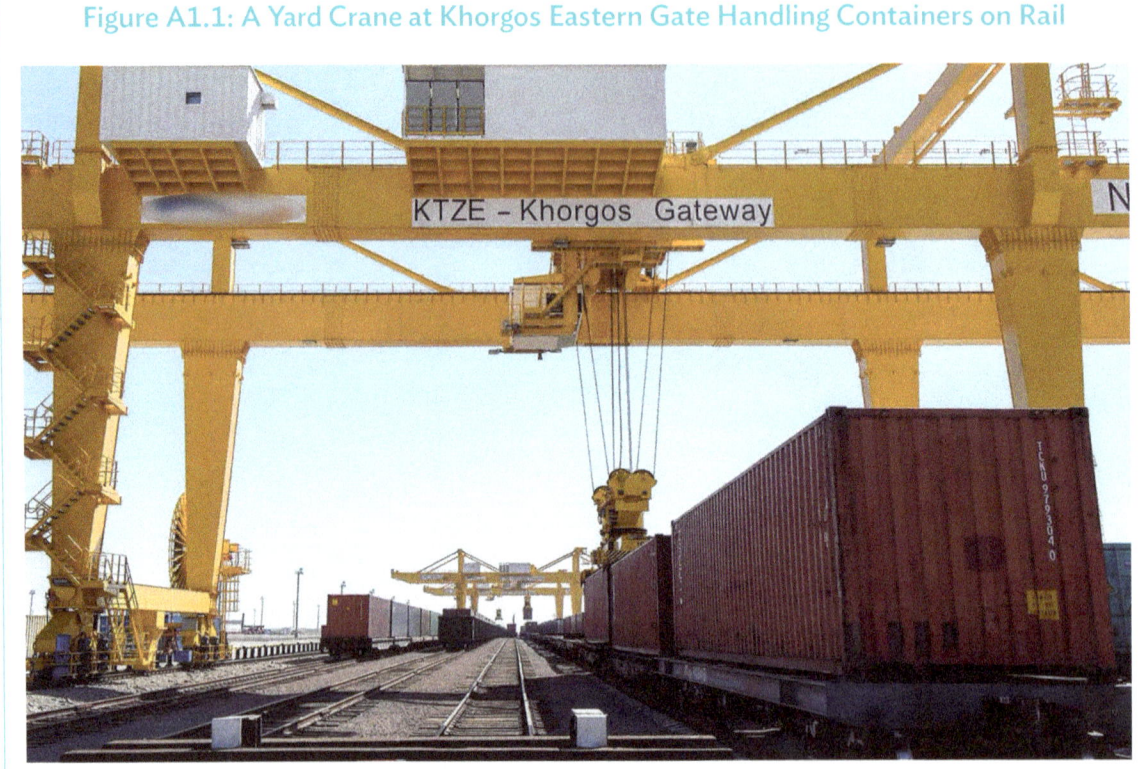

Source: Government of Kazakhstan. 2020. *Five-Year Results of Nurly Zhol Program: Construction of Toll Roads, Creation of New Jobs and Freight Traffic Growth*. Official Information Source of the Prime Minister of the Republic of Kazakhstan.

Figure A1.2: Nur Zholy Border-Crossing Point at Khorgos

Source: Government of Kazakhstan. 2020. *Five-Year Results of Nurly Zhol Program: Construction of Toll Roads, Creation of New Jobs and Freight Traffic Growth*. Official Information Source of the Prime Minister of the Republic of Kazakhstan.

Urumqi and Almaty are important origin and destination for bilateral trade. Almaty is also a consolidation center for the PRC shipments to Central Asia. A study using actual commercial shipments from Urumqi to Almaty, Bishkek, and Dushanbe compared the cost-effectiveness of trucking in these routes. The total freight rate and distance were recorded, and the two measures were split into the PRC and the Central Asian sections.

An analysis of the relationship between the freight rate and the distance according to the split found Kazakhstan to be proportionately more expensive than the Kyrgyz Republic and Tajikistan. For these two latter CARs, there was a perfect correlation between the proportion of road freight rate according to the distance in each country. Although the distance in Kazakhstan accounted for 36% of the total distance between Urumqi to Almaty, the road freight rate in the Kazakhstan section accounted for 52% (Table A1.5). This means trucking goods from Khorgos to Almaty appeared to be costlier.

Table A1.5: Comparing Road Freight Costs from the People's Republic of China to the Capital Cities of the Central Asian Republics

Routes	Distance			Road Freight		
Urumqi–Almaty	Total	PRC	KAZ	Total	PRC	KAZ
	665 km	63%	36%	$2,500	48%	52%
Kashi–Bishkek	Total	PRC	KGZ	Total	PRC	KGZ
	686 km	25%	75%	$2,600	25%	75%
Kashi–Dushanbe	Total	PRC	TAJ	Total	PRC	TAJ
	1307 km	20%	80%	$5,000	20%	80%

KAZ = Kazakhstan, KGZ = Kyrgyz Republic, km = kilometer, PRC = People's Republic of China, TAJ = Tajikistan.
Source: ADB (2019).

Dostyk and Altynkol, both located in Corridor 1 at the border with the PRC, are key railway BCPs. Both regular freight trains and dedicated container service to Europe pass through these BCPs. The shortage of wagons has consistently surfaced as a key delay at the border crossing. The magnitude of this delay is large relative to other delay reasons. Interestingly, CPMM samples revealed that the delay caused by wagon unavailability tended to peak in Q3 and Q4 from 2018 to 2020 (Figure A1.3).

This held true in 2020 as well, where the average delay in July to December rose quickly due to the resumption of manufacturing activities in the PRC, leading to a surge in demand for transportation and the diversion of freight to railways from road transport, which experienced restrictions in border crossings.

The problem associated with wagons is complicated and deserves a detailed explanation. The analysis led to a surprising conclusion: Kazakhstan does not suffer from a shortage of wagons. Instead, the deployment of wagons is not managed efficiently, leading to wagon deficits at places where they are needed. The problem must be traced back to the times of the Soviet Union to understand this. During that time, the Ministry of Communications oversaw the proper functioning of railways, and the national

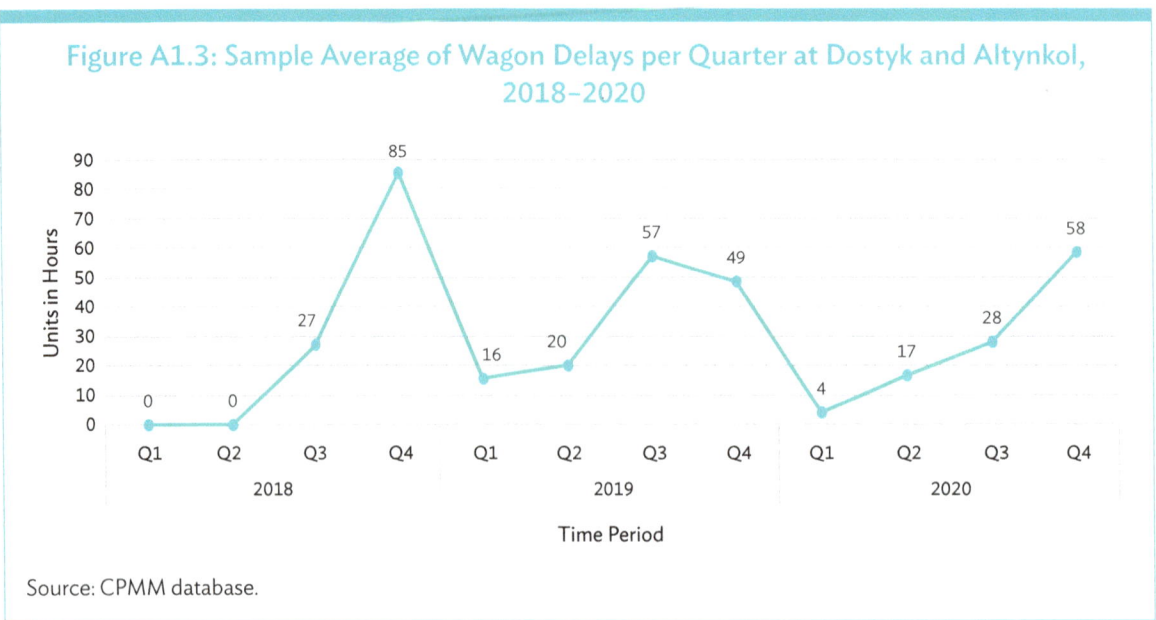

Figure A1.3: Sample Average of Wagon Delays per Quarter at Dostyk and Altynkol, 2018–2020

Source: CPMM database.

railway authority conducted the actual operation. Only two parties were involved, the shipper and the carrier. The shipper was the consignor and submitted the GU-12 form to apply for space on the railways for freight transport. The railway authority accepted the GU-12 form and aggregated all the requests for a particular month. The developed plan then directed the movement of empty and loaded wagons. The law mandated the railway authority to provide empty wagons and moved them to the designated station, while the consignor was responsible for loading the freight onto the wagon. The contract administration was simple then, with only two parties, and the roles and responsibilities were clear.

The dissolution of the Soviet Union disrupted this mechanism. Central planning no longer existed. Economic output dropped sharply, leading to excess wagons and other rolling stocks. At the onset of the new millennium, former Soviet Union states stabilized their economy; industrial production rose, creating demand for freight transport. Concurrently, the assets during the Soviet times had to be replaced due to natural wear and tear. This led to a shortage and prompted Kazakhstan to embark on a national reform for the railway sector, ushering in privatization. The outcome is that the national railway authority (Kazakhstan Temir Zholy or KTZ) transferred the assets to private owners (e.g., Kedentrans), which are now allowed by law.

New problems arose: which party is now responsible for securing the empty wagon, moving them to the designated stations, and loading the freight? If there is detention, who will pay for the penalty? On top of these issues, modern transport also resulted in external service providers, such as freight forwarders. This means the rail movement might require interactions between four parties—the consignor, the freight forwarder, the wagon owner, and the rail carrier. Kazakhstan is refining the Law on Railways by modernizing clauses related to these parties and their roles and responsibilities. Some recommendations are presented to ensure the efficient deployment of wagons: (i) standardizing contract formats between the stakeholders, (ii) encouraging long-term contracts between freight forwarders and wagon owners, and (iii) establishing wagon parks to hold idle wagons.

A fundamental principle is to modernize the railway sector to incentivize market-led practices, leading to higher wagon utilization. The privatization effort, while commendable, needs to be market-driven and correspond with demand. Otherwise, idle, empty wagons would lead to low returns on assets, additional shunting, and the need to build additional railway tracks to accommodate them. From 2010 to 2018, the compounded annual growth rate of private wagons grew at 7.98%, while the freight tonnage grew at 5.07%, and freight turnover increased only 3.62% (Table A1.6).

Table A1.6: Comparing the Annual Increase of Private Wagons versus Freight Demand Indicators

Comparisons	2010	2011	2012	2013	2014	2015	2016	2017	2018	CAGR
Privately Owned Wagons	43,305	51,924	61,192	63,477	71,351	73,177	72,848	75,496	80,050	7.98%
Freight Tonnage, mln. tons	267.9	279.7	294.8	293.7	390.7	341.4	338.9	387.2	397.9	5.07%
Freight turnover, mln. ton/km	213,219.0	223,626.0	235,892.9	231,289.5	280,653.8	267,362.2	238,972.2	266,611.9	283,345.2	3.62%

CAGR = compounded annual growth rate, mln. ton/km = million tons per kilometer.
Source: Government of Kazakhstan. Bureau of National Statistics. https://stat.gov.kz/official/industry/18/statistic/7 (accessed 13 August 2021).

A major delay happened at the BCPs on 15 November 2021, when the PRC authorities imposed new sanitation inspections and controls related to the COVID-19 pandemic. Each package of goods inside a container or wagon was unloaded and inspected for the coronavirus.

According to the bilateral railway agreement, the throughput allowed 18 trains per day. But this new measure reduced the throughput to 11 trains, with a low of 7 per day, impacting shipments of time-sensitive agricultural products and resulting in long queues of trains at the border.

Table A1.7 shows the country-level CPMM trade facilitation indicators for Kazakhstan from 2010 to 2020 for both road and rail transport. The average road-crossing time at Kazakhstan borders declined slightly from 9.5 hours in 2010 to 8.7 hours in 2020. The longer delays were observed at the Konysbaeva and Tazhen BCPs. Cost to cross a border declined from $296 to $123 over the period, but the cost to travel a corridor surged from $771 to $1,850. Trucks moved at relatively high average speeds within the country—52.9 km/h in 2020, compared with 48.8 km/h in 2010. However, the speed to travel through CAREC corridors was reduced to 29.2 km/h in 2020 from 30.4 km/h in 2010.

Rail freight faced longer delays than road cargo. The rail transport border-crossing time was already high in 2010 (36.7 hours), and it grew to 48.6 hours in 2020. Inbound shipments were the main source of longer delays. Rail border-crossing costs were higher than those for road transport and soared from $78 in 2010 to $341 in 2020. Slow border-crossing times negated some of the effect of higher average train speeds across Kazakhstan (up from 40.5 km/h in 2010 to 65.2 km/h in 2020) and lowered the overall transit speed to 15.3 km/h in 2020 from 33.7 in 2010.

Table A1.7: Kazakhstan—Trade Facilitation Indicators, 2010–2020

TFI	Road Transport	2010	2011	2012	2013	2014	2015	2016	2017	2018	2019	2020
TFI1	Time taken to clear a border-crossing point (hour)	9.5	7.4	9.8	6.0	3.6	3.8	4.4	8.6	7.1	9.2	8.7
	Outbound	*8.7*	*6.2*	*11.6*	*4.9*	*2.7*	*2.6*	*3.4*	*5.9*	*7.3*	*7.9*	*8.0*
	Inbound	*10.1*	*8.2*	*8.5*	*6.6*	*4.3*	*4.7*	*5.1*	*10.2*	*7.1*	*10.0*	*9.2*
TFI2	Cost incurred at border-crossing clearance ($)	296	216	170	138	105	104	113	124	96	115	123
	Outbound	*333*	*155*	*122*	*77*	*71*	*63*	*61*	*86*	*73*	*67*	*58*
	Inbound	*269*	*256*	*204*	*170*	*134*	*141*	*151*	*146*	*108*	*139*	*157*
TFI3	Cost incurred to travel a corridor section ($ per 500 km, per 20-ton cargo)	771	878	1,132	1,443	1,056	909	825	654	791	715	1,850
TFI4	Speed to travel on CAREC corridors (km/h)	30.4	32.8	30.1	31.2	31.0	30.6	31.5	28.8	30.5	30.7	29.2
SWOD	Speed without delay (km/h)	48.8	51.0	40.3	53.1	47.8	47.8	52.0	53.9	56.3	53.2	52.9

TFI	Rail Transport	2010	2011	2012	2013	2014	2015	2016	2017	2018	2019	2020
TFI1	Time taken to clear a border-crossing point (hour)	36.7	35.8	21.8	44.6	49.4	40.6	42.5	44.0	40.5	39.9	48.6
	Outbound	*6.8*	*11.1*	*9.9*	*10.0*	*15.8*	*15.6*	*16.1*	*15.6*	*7.8*	*9.0*	*8.4*
	Inbound	*43.9*	*42.1*	*26.8*	*58.5*	*51.8*	*44.1*	*46.9*	*48.4*	*49.2*	*46.7*	*56.2*
TFI2	Cost incurred at border-crossing clearance ($)	78	404	640	411	176	333	369	381	332	327	341
	Outbound	*–*	*–*	*7*	*95*	*96*	*116*	*115*	*117*	*122*	*122*	*124*
	Inbound	*78*	*404*	*803*	*447*	*182*	*364*	*411*	*421*	*358*	*351*	*356*
TFI3	Cost incurred to travel a corridor section ($ per 500 km, per 20-ton cargo)	278	254	484	1,044	1,256	1,107	929	808	768	687	724
TFI4	Speed to travel on CAREC corridors (km/h)	33.7	18.2	18.7	17.7	15.3	17.6	17.2	17.5	19.9	18.1	15.3
SWOD	Speed to travel on CAREC corridors (km/h)	40.5	39.4	43.2	40.9	40.4	51.8	53.6	57.2	56.4	67.8	65.2

CAREC = Central Asia Regional Economic Cooperation, km = kilometer, SWOD = speed without delay, TFI = trade facilitation indicator.

Source: CPMM database (unpublished).

Kyrgyz Republic

The Kyrgyz Republic is a landlocked, mountainous, lower-middle-income country with a population of 6.5 million. It borders Kazakhstan, Uzbekistan, Tajikistan, and the PRC. Corridors 1, 2, 3, and 5 pass through the Kyrgyz Republic. A mountain range separates the northern and southern parts of the country and bifurcates its economy.

The Kyrgyz Republic adopted a liberal trade regime after becoming a World Trade Organization (WTO) member in 1998. The country traditionally acted as an intermediary for manufactured goods trade, with its merchants profiting from transborder price differentials. The trade sector has been a driver of economic growth and employs about one-sixth of its population. Massive amounts of PRC-manufactured goods are re-exported to neighboring countries and the Russian Federation.

On 12 August 2015, the Kyrgyz Republic removed virtually all border controls after its official accession into the EAEU. The government also lifted phytosanitary controls on 19 November in the same year. Thus, only border security and veterinary inspections remained. Trucks crossed the border in a shorter time, e.g., at Ak Tilek–Kordai (Kyrgyz Republic–Kazakhstan), as no customs controls and phytosanitary inspections were at the borders.

Issues affected road freight, though. Kyrgyz trucks passed through Aul–Veseloyarsk (Kazakhstan–Russian Federation) smoothly but, at times, were subject to ad hoc and significant delays of 5 days or more. The Russian Federal Service for Veterinary and Phyto-Sanitary Surveillance detained trucks due to SPS reasons. The Kyrgyz Republic expected financial support from the Russian Federation to procure laboratory equipment, but this had not been given, constraining the Kyrgyz Republic's ability to comply fully with EAEU food safety standards. The Kara Suu Bazaar north of Osh and Dordoi Bazaar[8] north of Bishkek are among the largest in the region and frequented by traders from Kazakhstan, Uzbekistan, and Tajikistan. But sales at the Dordoi Bazaar and the Kara Suu Bazaar were both down significantly after the formation of the EAEU, even after the Kyrgyz Republic's accession in mid-2015.

Another issue was compliance with EAEU regulations. It was difficult to obtain a consensus on the transit guarantee provision. It was to be based on a surety amount that would be deducted if the agreed transit terms were violated. The Kyrgyz Republic operators considered the amount proposed by the Russian Federation too high and too onerous for its carriers, which are considerably smaller and less well resourced than the Russian Federation's carriers.

According to export statistics compiled by ADB, Kyrgyz export to Kazakhstan increased from $182 million in 2010 to $459 million in 2014, dropped to $228 million after its EAEU accession in 2015, and gradually climbed back to $338 million in 2019. Russian exports increased steadily from $258 million in 2010 to $271 million in 2019. Kyrgyz imports from the PRC increased from $3,225 million in 2010 to $4,904 million in 2019. Its import from the Russian Federation also surged from $666 million in 2010 to $1,735 million in 2019.

---

8   The Dordoi Bazaar is the largest trading hub between the PRC and Europe. Seventy-five percent of the goods sold at the Dordoi Bazaar and 85% of the goods sold at the Kara Suu Bazaar come from the PRC. Kazak [Author: Please note that the proper demonym should be "Kazakhstani." The term "Kazakh" is used to refer to ethnic Kazakhs, while the term Kazakhstani usually refers to all inhabitants or citizens of Kazakhstan, regardless of ethnicity.] traders bought some 70% of the goods from the Dordoi Bazaar before the creation of the EAEU but trailed off in 2014.

Road freight could also be subject to interferences from Kazakhstan. In March–April 2019, the Kazakhstan Revenue Committee initiated random checks at the Kyrgyz Republic–Kazakhstan BCPs, targeting Kyrgyz trucks carrying goods from the PRC. These very thorough checks encompassed detailed verification of documents and cargo, frequently leading to long lines and waiting times. The Kyrgyz Republic Freight Operators Association reported the extortion of unofficial payments connected to these checks. This matter was resolved only after extensive negotiations.[9]

Often, Kyrgyz import from the PRC does not match corresponding export statistics from the PRC. Some transporters reported that such activity has increased after the 2015 accession, as the Kyrgyz Republic received a very small share of the EAEU's customs revenue. Consequently, the Kazakhstan Revenue Committee organized periodic, random checks on goods carried by Kyrgyz trucks shortly after they entered Kazakhstan territory.

Table A1.8 shows the country-level CPMM trade facilitation indicators for the Kyrgyz Republic from 2010–2020 for road and rail transport.[10] CPMM data show that crossing the border by road has become more efficient since 2010. Border-crossing time improved from a relatively low of 3.9 hours in 2010 to 2.1 hours in 2020. Costs to cross a border also remained lower than the CAREC average of $199 and dropped from $54 in 2010 to $27 in 2020. However, overall transport costs, among the region's highest due to the country's mountainous terrain, rose from $974 in 2010 to $1,346 in 2020. Data showed improvements over the 2010–2020 period in both SWOD (from 35.3 km/h to 49.4 km/h) and speed with delay (SWD) (from 17.0 km/h to 26.9 km/h).

Table A1.8: Kyrgyz Republic—Trade Facilitation Indicators, 2010–2020

TFI	Road Transport	2010	2011	2012	2013	2014	2015	2016	2017	2018	2019	2020
TFI1	Time taken to clear a border-crossing point (hour)	3.9	6.1	5.6	3.3	1.1	2.8	3.4	3.5	1.6	1.6	2.1
	Outbound	*1.9*	*5.2*	*3.3*	*2.3*	*1.1*	*3.2*	*3.4*	*2.9*	*1.1*	*0.9*	*1.8*
	Inbound	*6.8*	*6.9*	*8.3*	*4.5*	*1.1*	*2.6*	*3.5*	*4.0*	*2.0*	*2.0*	*2.4*
TFI2	Cost incurred at border-crossing clearance ($)	54	121	80	114	35	71	142	121	24	23	27
	Outbound	*50*	*168*	*78*	*39*	*30*	*75*	*72*	*36*	*23*	*21*	*24*
	Inbound	*60*	*80*	*82*	*206*	*37*	*69*	*191*	*175*	*25*	*25*	*30*
TFI3	Cost incurred to travel a corridor section ($ per 500 km, per 20-ton cargo)	974	1,240	1,464	2,624	1,372	2,545	1,530	781	1,219	1,122	1,346
TFI4	Speed to travel on CAREC corridors (km/h)	17.0	16.3	22.5	21.2	24.5	23.5	26.2	28.1	29.8	30.8	26.9
SWOD	Speed without delay (km/h)	35.3	36.5	42.2	32.0	36.1	31.8	39.0	49.1	50.9	50.6	49.4

continued on next page

---

[9]   ADB. 2020. CAREC Corridor Performance Measurement and Monitoring Annual Report 2019. Manila.

[10]   CPMM does not capture extensive rail data from the Kyrgyz Republic to provide sufficient information on the trends.

Table A1.8   *continued*

TFI	Rail Transport	2010	2011	2012	2013	2014	2015	2016	2017	2018	2019	2020
TFI1	Time taken to clear a border-crossing point (hour)	–	–	2.9	–	–	–	–	–	1.2	1.2	1.7
	Outbound	–	–	–	–	–	–	–	–	–	–	–
	Inbound	–	–	*2.9*	–	–	–	–	–	*1.2*	*1.2*	*1.7*
TFI2	Cost incurred at border-crossing clearance ($)	–	–	49	–	–	–	–	–	–	–	–
	Outbound	–	–	–	–	–	–	–	–	–	–	–
	Inbound	–	–	*49*	–	–	–	–	–	–	–	–
TFI3	Cost incurred to travel a corridor section ($ per 500 km, per 20-ton cargo)	748	–	–	–	–	–	–	456	434	338	–
TFI4	Speed to travel on CAREC corridors (km/h)	7.6	–	–	–	–	–	–	35.9	21.6	23.5	16.2
SWOD	Speed to travel on CAREC corridors (km/h)	7.6	–	–	–	–	–	–	50.7	28.7	33.2	20.0

CAREC = Central Asia Regional Economic Cooperation, km = kilometer, SWOD = speed without delay, TFI = trade facilitation indicator.
Source: CPMM database (unpublished).

Mongolia

Mongolia is a landlocked country with two neighbors, the PRC, and the Russian Federation. Corridor 4 has three sub-corridors that serve as vital passageways for imports, exports, and transit shipments between the two neighboring countries.

Road freight carried slightly more than 30 million tons. Generally, it could account for 60% of all transported freight in 1 year, but the split between road and railways was even in 2020, as freight was diverted to the latter. Freight turnover was 19 billion ton-kilometers (ton-km) in 2020.[11] ADB has been an active partner in financing road rehabilitation and construction in Mongolia to promote regional integration and inclusive growth. A major achievement is the completion of the road section connecting Choir to Zamiin-Uud along Corridor 4. The completion signifies a new transit route in Corridor 4b and complements the transit by railways. Roads offer little transit potential between the Russian Federation and the PRC because the 1,000 km long railways linking Sukhbaatar to Zamiin-Uud traditionally conducted the transit. Moreover, the southern sections of the country did not have well-paved roads, which deterred any transit.

---

[11] Mongolian Statistical Information Service. *Transportation*. http://www.1212.mn/Stat.aspx?LIST_ID=976_L12&type=tables (15 June 2021).

The completion of the Choir to Zamiin-Uud road section, a 432 km two-lane carriageway paved with asphalt concrete, allows a new way to transport goods across the border besides using rail. For instance, automobiles from Yokohama in Japan and Pusan in the Republic of Korea were transported in containers by sea–rail to Zamiin-Uud. There, drivers then drove the automobiles from the border to Ulaanbaatar. This could be completed in 1–2 days compared to 5–7 days by train. The new road along Corridor 4b resulted in immediate improvement measured by CPMM. Using TFI3, which calculated the transport cost of a 20-ton shipment over 500 km, the cost of road transport has lowered from $1,437 to $1,200 (–16.45%). Speed has also increased; from 2013 to 2014, SWOD rose from 24 km/h to 36 km/h, a 50% increase.

Roads also play a role in other corridors. At Corridor 4a, coal from Mongolia is sent across Yarant BCP to the PRC processing plants. Minerals and ores from Oyu-Tolgoi and Tavantolgoi are trucked across Gashuunsukhait BCP to Inner Mongolia. At peak times when copper prices were high, a convoy of 500–600 trucks moved daily across this BCP. To promote greater regional connectivity and inclusive growth, ADB continues to finance the upgradation of infrastructure at remote locations, such as the $27 million modernization of the Bichigt and Borshoo BCPs. A longer-term plan may necessitate investment to build rail linkages between the PRC and Mongolia. This would reduce the shipment cost for bulk commodities as it is more economical to transport these items, such as copper, iron ores, and coal, using open-top wagons instead of trucks.

Rail freight carried close to 30 million tons (Table A1.9). Generally, it could account for 40% of all transported freight in 1 year, but the split between road and railways was quite even in 2020, as freight was diverted to the latter. Freight turnover was close to 24 billion ton-km in 2020.[12]

Table A1.9: Freight Tonnage and Turnover in Mongolia by Rail, 2017–2019

Indicator	2017	2018	2019	%
Carried freight, thousand tons	**22,765.1**	**25,763.3**	**28,143.0**	**100.00**
Domestic	9,484.6	10,326.8	11,091.1	39.41
Export	7,886.8	9,272.4	10,218.5	36.31
Import	2,302.7	2,798.4	2,937.8	10.44
Transit	3,091.0	3,365.7	3,895.6	13.84
Freight turnover, million ton-km	**13,493.2**	**15,315.3**	**17,384.1**	**100.00**
Domestic	2,473.5	2,866.3	3,153.8	18.14
Export	6,417.6	7,307.3	8,397.7	266.27
Import	1,171.1	1,405.8	1,508.5	17.96
Transit	3,431.0	3,736.0	4,324.1	286.65

Source: Mongolian Statistical Information Service. http://www.1212.mn/Stat.aspx?LIST_ID=976_L12&type=tables (accessed 13 August 2021).

---

[12]   National Statistics Office of Mongolia. Mongolian Statistical Information Service. *Transportation*. http://www.1212.mn/Stat. aspx?LIST_ID=976_L12&type=tables (accessed 13 August 2021).

Railways have always been the key mode of transport for international trade, maintaining a vital lifeline to imports and exports. Railways carried close to 30 million tons, of which exports contributed 10.2 million tons; imports, 2.9 million tons; and transit, 3.9 million tons in 2019. Export tonnage was 3.6 times that of import, and this pattern was similar to other CAREC countries. Exports from CAREC countries were bulky commodities with low value, such as raw commodities. Imports, on the other hand, especially from the PRC, were higher-value goods with lower volume or weight.

These essentially produced a phenomenon where the direction of trade is persistently imbalanced. The outbound trip required more wagons or containers than the inbound trip, thus, leading to higher shipping costs for exports. CPMM showed that a 20-foot container from Mongolia to Tianjin, a distance of 1,692 km, along Corridor 4b costs $1,800 compared to the import direction at $1,400, a 30% increase. This could impact export competitiveness, and there is no short-term action. Longer-term investments to achieve a higher-value migration (such as local value-added processing) and strengthening industrial linkages to produce an ecosystem would be instrumental so that the country could sell higher-unit value products instead of merely exporting raw materials.

ADB supported many initiatives to strengthen institutional capacity. A major accomplishment was the implementation of the Customs Automated Information System. Designed with three inputs, the project aimed to (i) update the system to an online environment with a central repository; (ii) finance inspection equipment and laboratory apparatus at key BCPs; and (iii) encourage public–private partnership, regional cooperation, and interagency coordination.

On cross-border cooperation, ADB promoted joint customs control between Mongolia and the PRC. An outcome is the use of a unified cargo manifest. This allows both Mongolian and Chinese shippers to declare their shipments using a standardized form. Under the principle of mutual recognition of controls, the inspection would only be conducted once and recognized by the other party. The unified cargo manifest was piloted in Zamiin-Uud and then expanded to the following BCPs after its success:

- Gashuunsukhait (Mongolia)–Gan Qimaodu (PRC)
- Shivee Khuren (Mongolia)–Ceke (PRC)
- Bichigt (Mongolia)–Zhu'engadabuqi (PRC)
- Khangi (Mongolia)–Mandula (PRC)

A challenge that has remained for the past decade is Mongolia's overreliance on Tianjin as its only gateway for foreign overseas trade. Its continued vulnerability due to this overdependence was highlighted when a 2015 explosion at a container storage station in the Binhai New Area of Tianjin disrupted the seaport's operations and delayed the country's shipments. Mongolia has been proposing a new rail connection from Ulaanbaatar to Chifeng in the PRC since 2015. This would link it to rail service to another northeast PRC seaport at Jinzhou. Little progress has been made on this idea so far.

"Transit Mongolia" Program

Transit Mongolia was launched in 2008 to

- expand Mongolia's role in transporting transit traffic between the PRC and the Russian Federation, and
- upgrade trade and transport facilitation measures to ensure its transport corridors will efficiently support import and export, especially mineral exports transported by rail

In addition to the existing main transport corridor (CAREC 4b), which government planners refer to as the Central Transit Corridor, they also envisaged expanding the railway network to include an Eastern Transit Corridor and a Western Transit Corridor. The two additional transit corridors would reduce transport distances for import and export traffic to and from eastern and western Mongolia and some transit traffic. The new transport corridors would also provide additional capacity to supplement the existing Central Transit Corridor.

Mongolia's 2010–2020 country-level CPMM road and rail transport trade facilitation indicators are shown in Table A1.10. The data indicates general efficiency in the country's road border-crossing processes. Crossing time increased from 3.8 hours in 2010 to 4.8 hours, but this was still low. Border-crossing costs dropped substantially from $334 over the period to $87 in 2020. CPMM also reveals a significant drop in transport costs, from $2,023 to $1,463. Truck shipment speed within the country remained relatively slow at 33.5 km/h in 2020. This was virtually unchanged from 33.3 km/h

Table A1.10: Mongolia—Trade Facilitation Indicators, 2010–2020

TFI	Road Transport	2010	2011	2012	2013	2014	2015	2016	2017	2018	2019	2020
TFI1	Time taken to clear a border-crossing point (hour)	3.8	4.5	5.9	6.0	6.7	2.9	2.3	3.2	3.5	3.7	4.8
	Outbound	2.7	3.4	5.5	5.5	3.3	1.6	1.3	2.9	2.9	2.9	1.5
	Inbound	4.5	5.0	6.0	6.3	7.7	3.2	2.5	3.2	3.5	3.7	5.0
TFI2	Cost incurred at border-crossing clearance ($)	334	286	356	622	383	138	89	93	93	97	87
	Outbound	53	18	22	31	92	113	63	12	13	12	27
	Inbound	562	328	397	839	453	144	94	104	104	109	90
TFI3	Cost incurred to travel a corridor section ($ per 500 km, per 20-ton cargo)	2,023	1,965	1,482	1,355	1,007	829	1,150	1,034	1,512	1,373	1,463
TFI4	Speed to travel on CAREC corridors (km/h)	19.3	19.3	19.7	16.4	22.6	28.8	29.4	28.5	33.5	26.2	24.4
SWOD	Speed without delay (km/h)	33.3	34.0	30.1	24.2	37.4	38.5	42.8	46.5	50.2	40.8	33.5

continued on next page

Table A1.10   *continued*

TFI	Rail Transport	2010	2011	2012	2013	2014	2015	2016	2017	2018	2019	2020
TFI1	Time taken to clear a border-crossing point (hour)	15.3	17.9	19.3	20.1	15.0	15.3	13.6	13.3	18.1	19.0	8.9
	Outbound	*11.7*	*11.9*	*9.3*	*12.7*	*3.1*	*4.3*	*6.7*	*7.6*	*11.7*	*8.7*	*2.1*
	Inbound	*20.1*	*24.6*	*27.6*	*24.9*	*21.1*	*21.3*	*17.7*	*16.6*	*20.4*	*21.4*	*10.6*
TFI2	Cost incurred at border-crossing clearance ($)	247	256	208	170	87	94	49	48	49	52	39
	Outbound	*301*	*320*	*315*	*240*	*86*	*78*	*75*	*–*	*27*	*11*	*6*
	Inbound	*52*	*137*	*135*	*131*	*87*	*97*	*45*	*48*	*49*	*54*	*51*
TFI3	Cost incurred to travel a corridor section ($ per 500 km, per 20-ton cargo)	484	476	430	862	1,307	1,412	835	827	1,030	720	852
TFI4	Speed to travel on CAREC corridors (km/h)	13.4	13.0	13.9	13.0	15.7	23.2	16.8	13.6	14.1	19.1	17.1
SWOD	Speed to travel on CAREC corridors (km/h)	21.1	23.5	26.4	27.5	32.9	43.6	32.2	22.7	20.9	24.1	21.5

CAREC = Central Asia Regional Economic Cooperation, km = kilometer, SWOD = speed without delay, TFI = trade facilitation indicator.

Source: CPMM database (unpublished).

in 2010, despite a brief spike to 50.2 km/h in 2018. Rail freight clearance time at Mongolia's border crossings increased steadily over much of the period, lengthening from 15.3 hours in 2010 to 19.0 hours in 2019, before dropping sharply to 8.9 hours in 2020 due to shorter time waiting for available wagons for inbound shipments at Zamiin-Uud. Costs for shipments to cross Mongolia's border by rail dropped during the 2010–2020 period from $247 to $39. Trains continued to move within Mongolia more slowly than in other CAREC countries. Average speeds barely rose from 21.1 km/h in 2010 to 21.5 km/h in 2020.

Pakistan

As one of the few countries with a developed maritime sector, Pakistan has 1,000 km of coastline and three seaports (Karachi, Port Said, and Gwadar) along the Arabian Sea and the Gulf of Oman. CAREC Corridors 3, 5, and 6 run through Pakistan and connect the seaports to Central Asia. However, Pakistan has borders with only two CAREC members, Afghanistan and the PRC, limiting the trade flows with the Central Asian republics (CARs) because transit through either neighbor country is not fully operational due to institutional barriers.

Road transport is the dominant mode of transport in Pakistan, accounting for 93%–96% of all freight traffic. The railway system handles mainly passenger traffic, although dedicated freight trains service commenced in 2019. The inland waterways, such as the Indus River, are not used currently for freight despite several studies indicating their potential. Air freight is also limited as most carriers focus on passengers, and Pakistan International Airlines undergoes a restructuring. The overreliance on road transport for freight resulted in a sustained high shipment, stress on the paved-road surface, and severe congestion, particularly at Karachi seaport and land BCPs.

A fundamental problem for road transport is the political organization of powers over roads. The 18th Amendment of the Constitution conferred regulatory powers to the provincial governments. This means that the provincial governments in the four provinces decide traffic permits, documentation, fees, etc., limiting any major decision by the federal body. At times, conflicts or implementation challenges could result if the federal government and the provincial authorities with whom the vehicles are registered do not agree. Another problem is the weak enforcement of vehicle specifications. There is a lack of engineering standards for locally produced vehicles, posing a safety hazard.

The direction of the freight movement is related to the country's geography; imports move from south to north because the imported goods enter primarily through the seaports in the south. Exports move mainly from north to south as the industrial centers, such as Faisalabad and Rawalpindi, are located inland and have to send the goods to the south. According to the observations of the Pakistan International Freight Forwarders Association, exports such as agricultural products, garments, and processed food are mainly low-unit-value items. Using road transport due to the unavailability of other transport modes means persistently high shipment costs. This is supported by CPMM data where Corridor 5 and the sections in Pakistan show relatively higher transport costs than other corridors.

Pakistan Railways covers 9,195 km of running tracks and another 2,686 km of sidings and loops—a total network of nearly 11,900 track km.[13] Of this network, approximately 87% has deferred track renewal work. ML-1 is the heart of the rail network that stretches 1,900 km in Karachi–Lahore–Islamabad–Peshawar. A double-track system exists between Karachi and Lahore that serves a target speed of 120 km/h and 23-ton axle load capacity. From Lahore onward, trains run on a single track with a target speed of 95 km/h with the same axle load capacity. Most of the rest of ML-1 operates at near capacity, particularly between Kotri and Rohri.

Rail freight rates are variable and depend on the demand versus supply situation. The rail freight rate shown includes the freight cost, lift-on/lift-off charges, terminal expenses, rail tariffs, and miscellaneous fees. The Ministry of Railways regulates rail pricing, and Pakistan Railways operates all rails.

During the implementation of the axle load regime, rail managed to attract more freight. This was because the average rail freight rate is PRs3,600 versus PRs6,000 per ton for road freight (60%).[14] Karachi–Lahore and Karachi–Faisalabad are the key cargo routes using rail and, to a lesser extent, Karachi–Multan. It costs $542–$606 to move one 20-foot container and $766–$830 for a 40-foot container from Karachi to Lahore based on recent surveys with Pakistan freight forwarders. Thus, it costs $4.00–$6.50 to move on rail at a per ton comparison.

---

[13]   The network includes 312 route kilometers of lightly used meter gauge lines.

[14]   At PR150 = $1 in 2019, average rail freight rate is $24 versus $40 per ton for road freight.

Rail transport has some key advantages over road freight, which is the dominant transport mode. First, worldwide, rail is cheaper than road transport. The payload for a boogie is 60 tons in Pakistan, and one train can move 30–35 boogies in one trip.

Second, barring exceptionally heavy storms, a train is considered "all-weather" and is less likely to be affected by climatic conditions, which can stop a truck, barge, or plane from operating.

Third, it is also a safer mode of transportation, and trains are less likely to be stopped at borders. This is a debatable point in Pakistan because train derailment accidents occur, and there is no rail connectivity with neighboring countries (in the future, rail transport will play an instrumental role under the China–Pakistan Economic Corridor).

Fourth, the private sector has long clamored for policies and incentives to move more freight on railways. A positive development is the freight train services that commenced in 2019, a joint effort by Pakistan Railways and National Logistics Cell. This service operates once per week between Karachi and Lahore. More freight train service can be expected, which will help offer more cost-competitive service for businesses.

A fundamental constraint in Pakistan is the absence of a unified ministry that oversees transportation. Different bodies develop policies and regulations, such as the Ministry of Road Transport, the Ministry of Maritime Affairs (formerly Ports and Shipping), the Ministry of Railways, and the Aviation Division. From 2018 to 2020, ADB, with the support of UKAid, provided technical assistance to develop the National Freight Logistics Policy for a unified framework to direct policy formulation and encourage multimodal transport. This aims to divert freight from road transport to lower shipment costs and efficiently enable goods to pass through different modes. The National Freight Logistics Policy is still pending review and approval by the Federal Cabinet.

Table A1.11 shows the country-level CPMM road transport trade facilitation indicators for Pakistan during 2011–2020. CPMM has recorded long delays at Pakistan BCPs. They averaged 55.7 hours in 2020. Torkham and Chaman have been among the most time-consuming BCPs, with performances further worsened by the effects of the pandemic. The cost to cross a border gradually increased from $202 in 2010 to $280 in 2020 (compared with the CAREC average of $199). Truck speeds within Pakistan reached a high SWOD of 70.3 km/h in 2012, but gradually declined to 28.1 km/h in 2020. Coupled with long delays at the border, the SWD in Pakistan was the lowest in the CAREC region in 2020 at 8.0 km/h.

Table A1.11: Pakistan—Trade Facilitation Indicators, 2010–2020

TFI	Road Transport	2010	2011	2012	2013	2014	2015	2016	2017	2018	2019	2020
TFI1	Time taken to clear a border-crossing point (hour)	–	5.1	39.5	36.2	33.5	29.9	37.2	56.9	36.3	38.2	55.7
	Outbound	–	*6.7*	*39.4*	*36.2*	*34.1*	*31.2*	*36.9*	*59.2*	*37.8*	*39.6*	*53.3*
	Inbound	–	*4.2*	*43.7*	*–*	*25.2*	*13.6*	*122.1*	*1.2*	*2.1*	*1.8*	*85.8*
TFI2	Cost incurred at border-crossing clearance ($)	–	202	289	230	245	290	287	280	282	283	280
	Outbound	–	*228*	*290*	*230*	*243*	*291*	*286*	*280*	*286*	*287*	*275*
	Inbound	–	*135*	*220*	*–*	*276*	*279*	*400*	*–*	*16*	*16*	*340*
TFI3	Cost incurred to travel a corridor section ($ per 500 km, per 20-ton cargo)	–	891	1,143	1,385	1,597	1,592	1,618	1,875	727	704	704
TFI4	Speed to travel on CAREC corridors (km/h)	–	4.7	17.7	16.8	17.5	21.3	18.9	9.8	13.7	10.6	8.0
SWOD	Speed without delay (km/h)	–	37.5	70.3	58.2	60.9	59.7	58.6	50.4	39.5	28.2	28.1

CAREC = Central Asia Regional Economic Cooperation, km = kilometer, SWOD = speed without delay, TFI = trade facilitation indicator.
Source: CPMM database (unpublished).

Tajikistan

Tajikistan is a landlocked country where 93% of the terrain is mountainous. This is advantageous for generating hydroelectric power, but challenging for physical transportation. Similar to the Kyrgyz Republic, the disintegration of the Soviet Union resulted in enclaves where roads and railways crisscrossed in neighboring countries. The country has a limited range of exports, such as aluminum and cotton. Corridors 2, 3, 5, and 6 traverse the country.

Freight by road is an essential service due to the disjointed railway system in Tajikistan. Truck shipments of agricultural products and commodities move across the Kyrgyz Republic and Uzbekistan to overseas markets. Before 2012, carriers could transport third-party goods across this BCP, but the Kyrgyz Republic authorities tightened enforcement in 2012–2013. Thus, goods originating or terminating outside the Kyrgyz Republic or Tajikistan could not cross Karamyk, resulting in alternative corridors to facilitate transit shipments.

The route via Karamyk (Route 1) was the traditional route for the shipment of goods from the PRC to Tajikistan and Afghanistan. However, at the end of 2012, the Kyrgyz Republic closed the border to international traffic; thus, trucks had to divert to cross the Batken BCP (Route 2). Another route was a transit corridor connecting the PRC, Tajikistan, and Afghanistan via the Kulma Pass (Route 3). While this avoided the need to cross the Kyrgyz Republic, the terrain is very mountainous, and heavy snow forced the BCP to close during the winter months.

Route 1 is the fastest and least costly. Route 2 is faster, while Route 3 is less costly (Table A1.12). Although Route 2 has two border crossings, the total time is still shorter. This is because of the mountainous terrain and the poor state of the uneven road surface along Route 3. This naturally acts as a speed limit to each truck traveling along Route 3. Thus, driving slowly at a farther distance result in an additional 1 or 2 days in Route 3. During the COVID-19 pandemic, the Kulma Pass reopened only on 30 May 2020 to allow trucks from the PRC to enter.

Table A1.12: Alternative Routes for Cargo Movement from Kashi to Dushanbe

Routes	Key BCP	Distance (km)	Time (hours)	Cost ($)
Route 1	Via Karamyk	877	80	$5,250
Route 2	Via Batken	1,198	105	$7,160
Route 3	Via Kulma Pass	1,307	121	$6,475

BCP = border-crossing point, km = kilometer.
Source: CPMM estimates.

Under Islam Karimov's former regime, Uzbekistan tended to institute an obstructionist policy, impeding cross-border trade. On 17 November 2011, Uzbekistan stopped railway traffic by closing the railway terminals at the Uzbekistan–Tajikistan border in the south. This interruption displaced 1,500–1,700 workers employed to operate the railways along the Kulyab–Kurgan Tyube–Kolkhozobod–Ayvad section in Tajikistan. Bilateral cooperation has improved since then under the new administration in Uzbekistan.

The Tajikistan railway is 670 km long. The rail gauge is 1,520 millimeters wide (broad). Divided into three sections, they are not interconnected and heavily rely on the Uzbekistan section of railways to move their goods. The railway is the primary mode used for exports, such as aluminum, cotton, and dried fruits. For imports, fuels and clay soil (for chemical production of aluminum) are transported on trains.

ADB promoted the Cross-Border Transport Agreement (CBTA) between Afghanistan, the Kyrgyz Republic, and Tajikistan. Technical assistance started in 2012 and ended in 2015 (ADB 2018). The initial objective was to promote greater regional trade by simplifying transit rules that would increase cross-border movement efficiency. One expected benefit was the shipment of goods in the PRC–Kyrgyz Republic–Tajikistan–Afghanistan along Corridor 5, from Kashi[15] to Dushanbe in Tajikistan or Shirkhan Bandar in Afghanistan. However, the lack of support from the PRC and the reluctance to designate Karamyk as an international BCP obstructed CBTA implementation. Karamyk is a road BCP designated by the Kyrgyz Republic Border Guard Service in 2007 to serve only bilateral traffic between the Kyrgyz Republic and Tajikistan. By 2014, the scope and funding for this technical assistance were reduced and concluded in 2015.

---

[15]   Kashi is also known as Kashgar, an important city in the ancient Silk Road located in southern Xinjiang Province in the PRC.

The 2010–2020 country-level CPMM road transport trade facilitation indicators for Tajikistan are in Table A1.13. The data illustrate the comparative efficiency of crossing the country's border by road during the period. An already low average border-crossing time of 7.8 hours in 2010 declined to 4.4 hours in 2020. Crossing costs remained substantially below the $199 CAREC average despite a slight increase from $71 to $90. On the other hand, despite improvements over the period in SWOD (from 19.9 km/h to 37.8 km/h) and SWD (from 18.5 km/h to 21.0 km/h), both underperformed the CAREC averages of 42.9 km/h (SWOD) and 22.7 km/h (SWD).

Table A1.13: Tajikistan—Trade Facilitation Indicators, 2010–2020

TFI	Road Transport	2010	2011	2012	2013	2014	2015	2016	2017	2018	2019	2020
TFI1	Time taken to clear a border-crossing point (hour)	7.8	4.4	3.2	3.5	4.7	4.6	4.3	3.8	3.8	4.3	4.4
	Outbound	*5.0*	*2.7*	*1.1*	*4.0*	*4.5*	*4.4*	*3.5*	*2.1*	*4.0*	*4.4*	*4.1*
	Inbound	*8.0*	*5.2*	*4.0*	*3.1*	*4.9*	*4.7*	*4.6*	*4.4*	*3.7*	*4.2*	*4.6*
TFI2	Cost incurred at border-crossing clearance ($)	71	129	133	74	69	144	142	103	118	105	90
	Outbound	*20*	*38*	*69*	*46*	*50*	*118*	*129*	*20*	*162*	*65*	*36*
	Inbound	*73*	*169*	*159*	*96*	*82*	*162*	*148*	*131*	*98*	*122*	*124*
TFI3	Cost incurred to travel a corridor section ($ per 500 km, per 20-ton cargo)	77	2,219	1,887	2,918	3,266	2,383	1,453	854	589	629	660
TFI4	Speed to travel on CAREC corridors (km/h)	18.5	21.4	18.6	21.8	21.3	22.1	21.3	23.1	23.3	22.5	21.0
SWOD	Speed without delay (km/h)	19.9	32.9	35.9	30.0	30.3	30.4	32.1	39.6	39.5	39.6	37.8

CAREC = Central Asia Regional Economic Cooperation, km = kilometer, SWOD = speed without delay, TFI = trade facilitation indicator.
Source: CPMM database (unpublished).

Turkmenistan

Most of Turkmenistan's existing railway traffic is domestic. Cross-border traffic (imports, exports, and transit traffic) is relatively small and accounts for about a quarter of freight volume. Corridors 2, 3, and 8 pass through Turkmenistan. The country shares a common border with Afghanistan, Kazakhstan, and Uzbekistan.

The new port has an annual throughput capacity of 17 million tons of cargo; 3 million tons of bulk cargo; 4 million tons of general cargo; 75,000 trucks; and 300,000 passengers (Figure A1.4).[16] In addition, the existing terminal for railway wagon ferries was also upgraded.

---

[16] Turkmenbashy International Seaport. 2018. Perception of New Opportunities. 5 August. https://turkmenistan.gov.tm/en/post/10539/turkmenbashy-international-seaport-perception-of-new-opportunities.

Figure A1.4: Turkmenbashy International Seaport

Source: Turkmenbashy International Seaport. General Cargo Terminal. https://port.com.tm/en/general-cargo-terminal/.

In January 2020, the government introduced reforms to separate the operation of freight and passenger railway services from the provision and management of railway infrastructure. The government created a new rail agency responsible for railway regulation, infrastructure, design and research, and training.

To improve the Turkmenbashi port for trade between Europe, the Caucasus, and Asia; and establish Turkmenistan as a regional trade and transit hub, Turkmenistan's main port on the Caspian Sea was upgraded in 2018 for around $1.5 billion. The new port section is rail-served and includes terminals for containers, general cargo, bulk cargo, automobiles, passengers, and facilities for serving polypropylene plants nearby. It also has a shipbuilding and repair yard. Reform and infrastructure enhancements should help Turkmenistan become a regional freight hub.

Table A1.14 shows the country-level CPMM trade facilitation indicators for Turkmenistan for 2010–2020 for road and rail transport. Road border-crossing time fell slightly from 8.8 hours in 2010 to 7.3 hours in 2020 and remained lower than the CAREC average of 15.1 hours. Border-crossing costs grew gradually over the period from $93 to $229 and exceeded the CAREC average of $199. The cost incurred to travel a corridor section in Turkmenistan was up to $1,029 in 2020 from $310 in 2010. Transit speeds were high, however, with CPMM showing the 2010 SWOD of 51.0 km/h further improving to 53.8 km/h in 2020. The data reflect efficiency in border crossing by train, with crossing times significantly reduced from 13.3 hours in 2013 to 5.7 hours in 2020. Border-crossing costs remained low—$151 in 2013, down to $87 in 2020. However, average train speed is comparatively low and gradually slowed from 40.0 km/h in 2014 to 28.2 km/h in 2020.

Table A1.14: Turkmenistan—Trade Facilitation Indicators, 2010–2020

TFI	Road Transport	2010	2011	2012	2013	2014	2015	2016	2017	2018	2019	2020
TFI1	Time taken to clear a border-crossing point (hour)	8.8	8.3	9.1	7.3	6.2	6.3	6.4	6.6	8.5	9.0	7.3
	Outbound	*10.0*	*9.6*	*8.8*	*7.1*	*5.6*	*5.9*	*5.8*	*5.8*	*7.4*	*7.5*	*8.9*
	Inbound	*8.3*	*7.3*	*9.4*	*7.5*	*6.7*	*6.6*	*6.8*	*7.1*	*9.1*	*10.0*	*6.9*
TFI2	Cost incurred at border-crossing clearance ($)	93	178	239	197	184	188	190	198	204	211	229
	Outbound	*89*	*93*	*62*	*56*	*58*	*70*	*58*	*60*	*62*	*63*	*65*
	Inbound	*95*	*242*	*370*	*298*	*272*	*274*	*281*	*300*	*284*	*302*	*311*
TFI3	Cost incurred to travel a corridor section ($ per 500 km, per 20-ton cargo)	310	625	739	702	719	740	763	748	1,017	1,094	1,029
TFI4	Speed to travel on CAREC corridors (km/h)	18.3	19.1	17.8	20.6	20.9	20.8	20.0	19.7	19.5	19.5	19.0
SWOD	Speed without delay (km/h)	51.0	47.7	47.6	52.6	51.1	51.3	51.5	51.7	53.9	54.3	53.8

TFI	Rail Transport	2010	2011	2012	2013	2014	2015	2016	2017	2018	2019	2020
TFI1	Time taken to clear a border-crossing point (hour)	–	–	–	13.3	12.0	4.6	4.2	5.4	3.3	3.5	5.7
	Outbound	*–*	*–*	*–*	*12.1*	*8.9*	*4.5*	*3.4*	*3.4*	*3.6*	*3.6*	*3.6*
	Inbound	*–*	*–*	*–*	*14.5*	*14.9*	*4.7*	*4.8*	*6.0*	*3.2*	*3.5*	*5.9*
TFI2	Cost incurred at border-crossing clearance ($)	–	–	–	151	158	128	100	73	94	97	87
	Outbound	*–*	*–*	*–*	*–*	*–*	*–*	*–*	*–*	*108*	*108*	*108*
	Inbound	*–*	*–*	*–*	*151*	*158*	*128*	*100*	*73*	*90*	*93*	*86*
TFI3	Cost incurred to travel a corridor section ($ per 500 km, per 20-ton cargo)	–	–	–	–	1,706	–	1,568	1,548	1,499	1,462	1,319
TFI4	Speed to travel on CAREC corridors (km/h)	–	–	–	–	9.6	–	9.9	13.7	14.1	14.0	13.7
SWOD	Speed to travel on CAREC corridors (km/h)	–	–	–	–	40.0	–	18.7	29.9	27.8	28.5	28.2

CAREC = Central Asia Regional Economic Cooperation, km = kilometer, SWOD = speed without delay, TFI = trade facilitation indicator.

Source: CPMM database (unpublished).

Uzbekistan

With a population of 34 million, Uzbekistan is the most populous country in Central Asia and well-positioned economically and technically. Among the former Soviet Union republics, Uzbekistan is one of the few that maintained a stable economy after the Soviet disintegration in 1991. Endowed with a good road and rail network, it is a key transit country in Central Asia. Its roadways and railway provide efficient connections with the road and rail system of Afghanistan, Iran, Kazakhstan, the Kyrgyz Republic, Tajikistan, and Turkmenistan. Corridors 2, 3, and 6 pass through Uzbekistan.

In 2016, Shavkat Mirziyoyev, who served for 13 years as Uzbekistan's prime minister, became president. Uzbekistan implemented many trade facilitation initiatives after Mirziyoyev became president. His 5 June 2020 decree No. UP-6005 "On Reforming Customs Administration and Improving the Activities of the State Customs Committee of the Republic of Uzbekistan" provided a road map for radical reforms of customs authorities and effective use of modern information and communication technologies by the customs service. He also issued another decree, "On Additional Measures to Ensure the Accelerated Development of Entrepreneurship, the Full Protection of Private Property, and the Qualitative Improvement of the Business Environment." This initiative sent a clear signal that the private sector would be the key driver for economic growth and job creation. The following year, Uzbekistan removed its foreign exchange controls, paving the way for foreign investments and international trade. Successes include attracting private capital to expand and modernize rail intermodal terminals (e.g., Chukursay), which are critical for UTY to grow its container traffic.

Adopting this decree improves the efficiency of customs service, including the formation of "digital customs," the development of paperless transactions, and accelerating the implementation of generally accepted international norms and standards. In addition, the endeavor will include "Risk Management System," "System for Automatic Registration and Distribution of Cargo Customs Declarations," "Customs Value Control System," and other comprehensive measures to simplify customs procedures. Further steps are being taken to speed up border inspection by streamlining workflow and equipping the BCPs with modern scanning equipment and smart systems.

Ultimately, this decree should transform the country's customs authorities into an enabler of trade, serving exporters and importers. Recognizing the importance of transportation to trade, Presidential Decree dated 1 February 2019 No. UP-5647 "On Measures to Fundamentally Improve the Public Administration System in the Field of Transport" established the Ministry of Transport to forge a unified transport policy, determine priorities for the transport and logistics industry, and develop international transport corridors. The creation of this ministry will help solve regional transport development issues. Also, Uzbekistan is working with its neighbors to promote trade.

In addition, to spur agricultural product exports, Uzbek business groups are working with the PRC buyers on developing e-commerce platforms to sell more products to the PRC. The governments of Kazakhstan and Uzbekistan are exploring the development of produce consolidation centers[17] to improve the logistics of exporting fresh produce to Kazakhstan.

---

[17] Uzbek farms are small and generally do not have enough volume to fill a whole refrigerated truck. Consolidation centers are highly beneficial in reducing shipping costs and in achieving sufficient scale to interest buyers.

Reform and Liberalization

An initiative to expand the throughput capacity of the Dustlik/Dostuk BCP at the border with the Kyrgyz Republic was launched. This is an important BCP for several reasons: (i) the export of Uzbekistan's produce; and (ii) the import of auto parts for the UzAuto Motor's plant at Asaka City, an important node of the Tashkent–Andijan–Osh–Irkeshtam–Kashgar route and the connecting point for the PRC–Kyrgyz Republic–Uzbekistan multimodal route. Since 2017, this BCP's operating hours have been expanded to 24/7, with major reconstruction planned for 2021. Also, a multimodal logistics center was built in nearby Andijan to function as a hub for rail and road transshipments.

Knowing the importance of road transportation to economic development and trade, the Uzbek government reduced the used truck tractor import tariff. It assisted road carriers in getting financing to grow their fleet. Such measures have significantly enlarged the Uzbekistan trucking industry, enabling its carriers to penetrate Western Europe, the Russian Federation, and CAREC countries like Georgia and Azerbaijan. In addition, the Ministry of Transport was created in 2019 to help develop Uzbekistan's transport and logistics sector.

The country's liberalization initiatives are already showing concrete results. More Fergana Valley BCPs are opened, operating hours lengthened, and controls loosened. Products from the PRC now move via the Kyrgyz Republic instead of through Kazakhstan. The BCPs along the Tajikistan border were reopened, and the rail link with Tajikistan reestablished. During a 2019 visit to Tashkent, a CPMM consultant witnessed Tajikistan cotton being containerized for export at Tashkent's main multimodal terminal.

Table A1.15 shows the country-level CPMM road and rail transport trade facilitation indicators for Uzbekistan for 2010–2020. Road border-crossing time jumped to 10.1 hours in 2020 from 6.4 hours in 2010 due to longer and more stringent inspections for health and quarantines. The average road border-crossing cost declined slightly over the period from $151 to $102. Truck shipment speeds within Uzbekistan were largely unchanged, but still faster than the CAREC averages. SWOD was 49.6 km/h in 2020 (CAREC—42.9 km/h), and SWD was 26.6 km/h (CAREC—22.7 km/h). Data indicated efficiency in border crossings by train. The rail border-crossing time average gradually declined from 10.9 hours in 2013 to 6.4 hours in 2020. Crossing costs remained moderate at $125 in 2020, although up from $82 in 2013. Train speeds are quite a bit lower than the CAREC average of 42.2 km/h, however, though improved in 2020 to 21.9 km/h from 12.7 km/h in 2010.

Table A1.15: Uzbekistan—Trade Facilitation Indicators, 2010–2020

TFI	Road Transport	2010	2011	2012	2013	2014	2015	2016	2017	2018	2019	2020
TFI1	Time taken to clear a border-crossing point (hour)	6.4	6.9	11.0	7.2	5.9	5.9	5.9	5.8	8.5	7.7	10.1
	Outbound	*6.8*	*6.7*	*12.3*	*8.2*	*6.0*	*5.9*	*5.9*	*5.6*	*8.5*	*7.8*	*7.6*
	Inbound	*5.6*	*7.3*	*9.4*	*5.6*	*5.7*	*5.8*	*6.0*	*6.1*	*8.5*	*7.7*	*14.0*
TFI2	Cost incurred at border-crossing clearance ($)	151	160	243	51	78	89	99	88	73	87	102
	Outbound	*101*	*121*	*132*	*38*	*74*	*81*	*91*	*80*	*66*	*92*	*124*
	Inbound	*182*	*196*	*342*	*56*	*81*	*96*	*108*	*96*	*80*	*83*	*83*
TFI3	Cost incurred to travel a corridor section ($ per 500 km, per 20-ton cargo)	337	424	468	447	508	445	426	423	477	600	648
TFI4	Speed to travel on CAREC corridors (km/h)	28.5	27.6	28.8	28.5	29.4	29.4	28.5	28.0	28.5	28.6	26.6
SWOD	Speed without delay (km/h)	46.8	46.2	39.5	50.4	50.6	49.3	47.6	46.8	50.8	49.6	46.9

TFI	Rail Transport	2010	2011	2012	2013	2014	2015	2016	2017	2018	2019	2020
TFI1	Time taken to clear a border-crossing point (hour)	12.0	–	–	10.9	7.4	10.5	9.4	7.5	5.6	6.2	6.4
	Outbound	*–*	*–*	*–*	*17.2*	*13.9*	*15.4*	*15.8*	*15.5*	*11.1*	*14.0*	*14.0*
	Inbound	*12.0*	*–*	*–*	*4.9*	*0.8*	*5.7*	*3.5*	*2.7*	*3.6*	*4.0*	*5.2*
TFI2	Cost incurred at border-crossing clearance ($)	–	–	–	82	95	97	103	112	112	113	125
	Outbound	*–*	*–*	*–*	*93*	*95*	*99*	*103*	*98*	*99*	*99*	*100*
	Inbound	*–*	*–*	*–*	*71*	*–*	*95*	*104*	*120*	*118*	*119*	*129*
TFI3	Cost incurred to travel a corridor section ($ per 500 km, per 20-ton cargo)	476	520	201	1,378	1,866	1,710	1,409	1,138	971	778	671
TFI4	Speed to travel on CAREC corridors (km/h)	12.0	8.7	23.8	8.5	8.1	10.4	10.8	10.0	14.0	10.5	9.7
SWOD	Speed to travel on CAREC corridors (km/h)	12.7	8.7	23.8	39.5	39.7	41.6	36.5	25.3	27.9	38.2	21.9

CAREC = Central Asia Regional Economic Cooperation, km = kilometer, SWOD = speed without delay, TFI = trade facilitation indicator.

Source: CPMM database (unpublished).

CAREC Regional Average Trade Facilitation Indicators

Table A1.16 presents the average road and rail trade facilitation indicators for the CAREC region from 2010–2020. During this period, the average border-crossing time at borders along CAREC corridors deteriorated from 6.3 hours to 15.1 hours. A jump in the average time was evident in 2014 when data for Pakistan borders were included in the sample as the country joined CAREC. The slight improvement in the indicator in 2018 and 2019 was negated in 2020, largely due to the stricter border-crossing procedures to curb the spread of the pandemic. The average border-crossing cost was largely unchanged from $192 in 2010 to $199 in 2020, but with abrupt fluctuations in between. Analysis in Chapter 2 suggests that, upon adjusting for inflation, the cost indicator has remained

Table A1.16: CAREC—Trade Facilitation Indicators, 2010–2020

TFI	Road Transport	2010	2011	2012	2013	2014	2015	2016	2017	2018	2019	2020
TFI1	Time taken to clear a border-crossing point (hour)	6.3	6.2	8.8	5.6	9.9	9.3	11.3	16.9	12.0	12.2	15.1
TFI2	Cost incurred at border-crossing clearance ($)	192	150	145	236	177	149	160	159	155	162	199
TFI3	Cost incurred to travel a corridor section ($, per 500km, per 20-ton cargo)	758	1,093	1,068	1,596	1,359	1,341	1,174	947	953	901	918
TFI4	Speed to travel on CAREC Corridors (kmph)	24.4	24.2	25.9	22.3	22.9	23.2	22.3	22.2	23.4	22.6	22.7
SWOD	Speed without Delay (kmph)	41.0	43.0	39.4	37.8	42.0	40.2	41.7	45.0	46.3	43.6	42.9

TFI	Rail Transport	2010	2011	2012	2013	2014	2015	2016	2017	2018	2019	2020
TFI1	Time taken to clear a border-crossing point (hour)	22.1	26.1	25.3	29.9	32.6	27.4	25.9	26.2	23.2	20.6	23.0
TFI2	Cost incurred at border-crossing clearance ($)	160	265	280	229	148	208	215	202	196	198	193
TFI3	Cost incurred to travel a corridor section ($, per 500km, per 20-ton cargo)	464	344	468	911	1,364	1,250	966	976	970	820	836
TFI4	Speed to travel on CAREC Corridors (kmph)	22.3	14.6	14.8	13.3	11.4	14.0	14.3	14.8	15.9	19.0	16.8
SWOD	Speed without Delay (kmph)	27.2	30.1	34.4	31.7	32.2	38.3	38.6	37.6	35.4	45.0	42.2

CAREC = Central Asia Regional Economic Cooperation, km = kilometer, SWOD = speed without delay, TFI = trade facilitation indicator.

Source: CPMM database (unpublished).

relatively stable in real terms, especially since 2015. The SWOD improved from 41.0 km/h in 2010 to 42.9 km/h in 2020. However, the gains in speed were offset by long delays at the border, resulting in deterioration in SWD from 24.4 km/h in 2010 to 22.7 km/h in 2020.

For rail transport, the border-crossing time remained consistently lengthy from 22.1 hours in 2010 to 23 hours in 2020. As described in individual country performances, the high average border-crossing time was partly attributed to long delays of inbound trains in Kazakhstan due to unavailable wagons. On average, rail border-crossing cost rose from $160 in 2010 to $193 in 2020 in the CAREC region. Train speeds rose from 27.2 km/h in 2010 to 42.2 km/h in 2020. However, similar to road transport, the improvement in speeds was negated by long border clearance procedures, reversing the progress in SWD from 22.3 km/h in 2010 to 16.8 km/h in 2020.

COVID-19 RESPONSES IN CAREC

T he Central Asia Regional Economic Cooperation (CAREC) Program conducted a comprehensive survey with the Corridor Performance Measurement and Monitoring (CPMM) partners in 2020 to understand the temporary measures imposed by each country and the associated impacts. The following summarizes the strict measures adopted by each CAREC country at the beginning of the pandemic to combat the spread of coronavirus disease (COVID-19).

Afghanistan

At the onset, all international border-crossing points (BCPs) ceased operation. Torkham and Spin Buldak reopened 3 days per week and gradually increased to 6 days per week in June 2020. The average waiting time to cross Torkham surged from 6.7 hours in March to 24.5 hours in April and remained elevated in May and June 2020. In June 2020, civil unrest at the Khojak Pass stopped traffic at the Chaman BCP.

Azerbaijan

The Government of the Republic of Azerbaijan allowed foreign freight vehicles to enter or transit through the territory of Azerbaijan. All BCPs with Iran, Georgia, the Russian Federation, and Türkiye were open for foreign trucks. However, Azerbaijan mandated that Iranian trucks transiting through Azerbaijan's territory to and from Georgia must be escorted by police. Maritime transportation with Turkmenistan and Kazakhstan is also open under certain restrictions wherein drivers are tested in the Port of Baku before loading.

People's Republic of China

The Khorgos International Center of Boundary Cooperation was temporarily closed on 24 January 2020 and reopened on 19 March, while all the People's Republic of China (PRC) BCPs with Kazakhstan remained open for road and rail freight (Khorgos/Alashankou) traffic. The Torugart and Irkeshtam BCPs with the Kyrgyz Republic were closed on 6 February 2020, but subsequently reopened. Pakistan closed its border with the PRC throughout the first half of 2020, but resumed the operations of the Khunjerab Pass BCP on 5 August 2020. The Kulma Pass BCP with Tajikistan remained open.[1] The Erenhot BCP with Mongolia remained open, while Takashikent is open only for certain cargo under special handling procedures.

---

[1]   However, the PRC trucks cannot enter Tajikistan. Cargo must be transferred to Tajik trucks at the border.

Georgia

The government launched a coordinated and comprehensive set of measures to combat the pandemic. These measures—work from home and issuance of documents—covered controls to impede the spread of COVID-19 and support measures for industries. Notwithstanding, the pandemic still impacted Georgia in terms of shipment times. The surge was caused by isolated incidents: (i) incoming shipments in May from Türkiye into Georgia at Sarpi, where drivers waited 24 hours to cross the border; (ii) drivers with suspected symptoms being quarantined at Tsiteli Khidi for 5 days; and (iii) restrictions imposed by other countries, delaying the entry of goods at Sarpi. Otherwise, the border crossing at Georgian BCPs was faster due to lower-than-normal traffic.

High-traffic BCPs at Tsiteli Khidi and Sarpi remained fully open throughout the first half of 2020. General measures adopted at all BCPs included temperature screening of drivers, truck disinfection, and quarantine imposed on drivers from "Red Zone Countries." Foreign drivers must exit Georgia within 96 hours (4 days), except those for a return haul operation or waiting to board a ferry, in which case they can stay up to 7 days.

Kazakhstan

High-traffic BCPs at Dostyk and Altynkol remained fully open throughout the first half of 2020. These two BCPs facilitated both road and rail transport. For a limited period, all Kazakhstan road BCPs were closed. All freights were diverted to rail transport. However, congestion at Alashankou and Khorgos led to a suspension of freight movements to those BCPs from 17 to 24 June, except container express trains to Europe and Central Asia.

From mid-May until June, the presence of tax and customs authorities at the Kazakhstan BCPs such as Karasu (Kazakhstan–Kyrgyz Republic) resulted in strict measures that increased shipment costs. Due to the additional control measures, a truck has to wait 3–6 days. Kyrgyz truck operators had to resort to unofficial payments amounting to $300–$2,500 per truck to expedite. Thus, the increase in shipment cost is reflected in Trade Facilitation Indicator 3 (TFI3) for the second quarter.

Kyrgyz Republic

In response to COVID-19, the Government of the Kyrgyz Republic declared a state of emergency on 25 March 2020, around the same time as its Central Asian neighbors. Additional checks and controls were introduced at the BCPs, but they remained mostly open.[2] Transit agreements were struck with Kazakhstan, Tajikistan, and Uzbekistan for Kyrgyz trucks to continue delivering cargo to these countries and transit through them. However, the border-crossing time increased substantially. For example, crossing into Uzbekistan at the Dostuk BCP rose from 0.6 hours (first half 2019) to 1.6 hours (first half 2020). Likewise, the border-crossing time at Ak-Tilek BCP with Kazakhstan increased

---

[2]   The Torugart BCP with the PRC is still closed, but the Irkeshtam BCP is open.

from 0.1 hour to 0.4 hour for outbound shipments and 0.1 hour to 0.7 hour for inbound shipments over the same period.

Compliance with stringent sanitary standards, disinfection, and health and quarantine checks increased transport time and costs, significantly raising the operating costs of Kyrgyz road carriers. In addition, a significant amount of cargo was shifted to rail since the start of COVID-19. As a result, this pandemic has placed the Kyrgyz trucking industry, mostly small and medium-sized operators, under stress.

Mongolia

The State Special Commission announced general measures to stall the spread of COVID-19 on 10 February 2020. The General State Inspection Agency ordered disinfection and other measures on 13 March 2020. No restriction was enforced on the domestic movement of people and freight. The Mongolia Customs General Authority determined that selected items would need to be handled and cleared at inland customs offices. Items under this list included raw and processed meat. As such, bonded carriers would be activated to escort the truck to the inland customs offices. Since all commercial airlines were canceled during the pandemic, air carriage capacity for flying goods in and out of Mongolia was severely reduced. This diverted freight to land-based transportation.

High-traffic BCPs at Zamiin-Uud and Sukhbaatar remained fully open throughout the first half of 2020. Road BCPs at Altanbulag, Borshoo, and Zamiin-Uud continued operations. However, Bichigt was not operational as the PRC closed the adjacent border. During the epidemic, freight flow remained open, but the borders were closed to the passage of passengers. The PRC trucks could not enter Mongolia, so goods must be transloaded in designated areas to Mongolian trucks.

Pakistan

The government has ordered a moratorium on all cross-border activities since early March 2020, resulting in a stoppage of all border activities at the Torkham and Chaman BCPs. Thus, many containers bound for Afghanistan were stuck at the seaport, inland customs offices, and two BCPs. By 14 March 2020, the Pakistan Customs reported that 1,587 containers and 526 containers remained in Quetta and Peshawar, respectively, after being released from the Karachi seaport. In the meantime, the containers' seals were intact and stayed in the customs-bonded zone. By 22 April 2020, the Pakistan International Freight Forwarders Association estimated that 6,000 twenty-foot equivalent units (TEUs) bound for Afghanistan were stuck in Karachi's seaport.

The strict measures to contain the outbreak led to economic hardships; the government reviewed and adopted countermeasures. In April, the Ministry of Interior ordered a partial reopening and resumption of 6-day operations in May 2020 for Torkham and Chaman. The Directorate General of Transit Trade agreed to waive demurrage and detention charges on containers held in Pakistan to provide temporary relief for the shippers and transport operators.

Tajikistan

The government designed the provisional procedure for regulating international transit as ordered by the president on 16 March 2020 (No. 1k/25-2) and the prime minister (No. 2k/20-25) under the prevention framework against COVID-19 in Tajikistan. The Ministry of Transport approved the "Temporary Regulation of International Freight Road Transport in Tajikistan" on 2 April 2020. This regulation applies to the import, export, and transit of goods.

High-traffic BCPs at Bratsvo, Fotehobod, and Guliston were operational throughout the crisis. The Kulma Pass was closed on 20 March and reopened on 30 May 2020. This Kulma BCP is located at the Tajik–PRC border and was halted partly due to winter and high altitude and partly to halt the spread of COVID-19 from the PRC. There was no abrupt or severe impact on the trade facilitation indicators (TFIs).

Turkmenistan

The Government of Turkmenistan closed its borders to foreign trucks on 23 March 2020. Subsequently, the Garabogaz BCP (at the Kazakhstan border) and the Farap BCP (at the Uzbekistan border) were reopened. But shipments entering Turkmenistan must be transloaded from foreign trucks into Turkmen trucks without contact at designated areas at the border.

Foreign trucks arriving in Turkmenbashy International Seaport on 23 March 2020 or earlier can leave their trailers or semitrailers in the designated areas of the port for pick up by Turkmen carriers for in-country delivery or transit through its territory. Afterward, foreign tractors must return, with the driver, by sea to the originating port. But after 23 March 2020, all cargoes to Turkmenbashy Port must be sent in trailers or semitrailers without tractors and drivers. Turkmenistan essentially shut its borders to foreign trucks, as foreign carriers cannot forge interline agreements with Turkmen carriers (to which they can entrust both the cargo and equipment) during such a short adjustment period.

Uzbekistan

Uzbekistan closed its border on 15 March 2020 after the first COVID-19 case was detected. It subsequently reopened its borders to freight traffic under strict health and quarantine controls. All national and foreign drivers must pass the COVID-19 testing procedure, which takes about 14–16 hours for the results. There was no charge for such a test. Drivers stayed at special Uzbek parking areas near the BCPs while awaiting test results. Basic services were provided to drivers, and special personnel had access to such areas.

Additional time and costs associated with enhanced health screening, quarantine, and sanitization have increased the operating costs of Uzbek carriers. At the same time, demand and supply imbalance prevented them from passing the cost increases to shippers, squeezing their already thin profit margin. Consequently, COVID-19 has negatively impacted the Uzbek road transport sector, causing some carriers to suffer financial difficulties.

REFERENCES

Asian Development Bank (ADB). 2014. *CAREC Corridor Performance Measurement and Monitoring: Annual Report 2014*. Manila.

———. 2017. *Country Partnership Strategy: Afghanistan, 2017–2021—Achieving Inclusive Growth in a Fragile and Conflict-Affected Situation*. Manila. https://www.adb.org/sites/default/files/institutional-document/371531/cps-afg-2017-2021.pdf.

———. 2018. *Technical Assistance Completion Report: Facilitating Cross-Border Transport in the Central Asia Regional Economic Cooperation Region (Phase 1)*. Manila. https://www.adb.org/sites/default/files/project-documents/46274/46274-001-tcr-en.pdf.

———. 2019. *CAREC Corridor Performance Measurement and Monitoring: Annual Report 2018*. Manila.

———. 2020. *CAREC Corridor Performance Measurement and Monitoring: Annual Report 2020*. Manila.

———. 2021. *E-commerce in CAREC Countries: Laws and Policies*. Manila. https://www.adb.org/sites/default/files/publication/725671/E-commerce-carec-laws-policies.pdf.

U. Aydin. 2020. Barriers and Solutions to Economic Integration of Caspian Sea Countries. *ADBI Working Paper Series* No. 1108. April. Tokyo: ADB Institute. https://www.adb.org/sites/default/files/publication/579731/adbi-wp1108.pdf.

P. Coke-Hamilton. 2019. *We Must Help Developing Countries Escape Commodities Reliance*. World Economic Forum. https://www.weforum.org/agenda/2019/05/why-commodity-dependence-is-bad-news-for-all-of-us/.

Z. Drabek and S. Laird. 2001. Can Trade Policy Mobilize Financial Resources for Economic Development? *Staff Working Paper* No. ERAD-2001-02. August. World Trade Organization. https://www.wto-ilibrary.org/economic-research-and-trade-policy-analysis/can-trade-policy-help-mobilize-financial-resources-for-economic-development_4cf4d332-en.

The Economist. 2020. How COVID-19 Put Wind in Shipping Companies' Sails. 10 October. https://www.economist.com/business/2020/10/10/how-covid-19-put-wind-in-shipping-companies-sails.

European Commission. *Mobility and Transport: Road Safety*. https://road-safety.transport.ec.europa.eu/eu-road-safety-policy/priorities/safe-road-use/safe-speed/archive/current-speed-limit-policies_en.

Eurasian Economic Commission. 2015. *The Treaty on the Eurasian Economic Union Is Effective*. http://www.eurasiancommission.org/en/nae/news/Pages/01-01-2015-1.aspx.

Eurasian Economic Union. General Information. http://www.eaeunion.org/?lang=en#about-info.

Y. Kalyuzhnova and H. Holzhacker. 2021. Enhancing Connectivity and Trade Between Central Asia Regional Economic Cooperation Countries and the World: Benefits, Risks, and Policy Implications. *ADBI Working Paper Series* No. 1271. June. Tokyo: ADB Institute.

M. Lee. 2020.Five Keys to Expanding Central Asia's Global Value Chains. *Asian Development Blog*. 26 November. https://blogs.adb.org/blog/five-keys-to-expanding-central-asia-global-value-chains.

Middle Corridor. History. https://middlecorridor.com/en/about-the-association/history-en.

Mongolian Statistical Information Service. *Transportation*. National Statistics Office of Mongolia. http://www.1212.mn/Stat.aspx?LIST_ID=976_L12&type=tables (accessed 15 June 2021).

R. Pomfret. 2019. *The Central Asian Economies in the Twenty-First Century: Paving a New Silk Road*. New Jersey: Princeton University Press.

J. Sachs. 2005. *The End of Poverty*. London: Penguin Press.

Turkmenistan Golden Age. 2018. Turkmenbashy International Seaport: Perception of New Opportunities. 5 August. hhttps://turkmenistan.gov.tm/en/post/10539/turkmenbashy.

United Nations Conference on Trade and Development (UNCTAD). 2016. Trade Facilitation and Development: Driving Trade Competitiveness, Border Agency Effectiveness and Strengthened Governance. *Transport and Trade Facilitation Series* No. 7. UNCTAD. https://unctad.org/system/files/official-document/dtltlb2016d1_en.pdf.

J. Wilson, C. Mann, and T. Otsuki. 2005. *Assessing the Benefits of Trade Facilitation: A Global Perspective*. Blackwell Publishing. https://artnet.unescap.org/tid/artnet/mtg/gravity10_reading2.pdf.

World Bank. Doing Business. https://www.doingbusiness.org/en/data/exploreeconomies (accessed 13 August 2021).

World Trade Organization. *Trade facilitation*. https://www.wto.org/english/tratop_e/tradfa_e/tradfa_e.htm.

Lightning Source UK Ltd.
Milton Keynes UK
UKHW020410160223
417096UK00035B/534